BEGINNER'S
Houseplant
Garden

BEGINNER'S
Houseplant
Garden

Top 40 Choices for Houseplant Success & Happiness

JADE MURRAY

CREATIVE
HOMEOWNER®

To my three children, Jayden, Kamil, and Aurora-Mary,
who have been my driving force throughout life.

If Jayden were a plant, he would be a jade plant. If Kamil were
a plant, he would be a string of dolphins. And if Aurora-Mary
were a plant, she would be a *Philodendron* 'Pink Princess.'

CRE⌂TIVE
HOMEOWNER®

Creative Homeowner® is a registered trademark of New Design Originals Corporation.

Originally published in the United Kingdom in 2022 as The Indoor Garden
Copyright Pimpernel Press Ltd 2022
Text copyright Jade Murray 2022
Illustrations copyright Jade Murray 2022

Beginner's Houseplant Garden
Managing Editor: Gretchen Bacon
Copy Editor: Christa Oestreich
Designer: Wendy Reynolds

Images used from Shutterstock.com: Rawpixel.com (front cover), Cheng Wei (82 inset).

ISBN 978-1-58011-593-3

Library of Congress Control Number: 2022946001

We are always looking for talented authors. To submit an idea, please send a brief inquiry to acquisitions@foxchapelpublishing.com.

Printed in China

Current Printing (last digit)
10 9 8 7 6 5 4 3 2 1

Creative Homeowner®, *www.creativehomeowner.com*, is an imprint of New Design Originals Corporation and distributed exclusively in North America by Fox Chapel Publishing Company, Inc., 800-457-9112, 903 Square Street, Mount Joy, PA 17552, and in the United Kingdom by Grantham Book Service, Trent Road, Grantham, Lincolnshire, NG31 7XQ.

Contents

PAGE 1 *Begonia maculata* (polka dot begonia)
PAGE 2 *Calathea lancifolia* (rattlesnake plant),
Calathea Medallion; *Calathea makoyana* (peacock plant)
LEFT *Dracaena trifasciata* (snake plant)

Introduction

With a little bit of time, care, and attention, I believe we can all reap the benefits of what indoor plants have to offer. Plant care is self-care as they contribute to our peace of mind.

I might have grown up in the city, but I have always been a nature girl at heart—appreciating the forever-changing sky, the leaves on trees blowing in the wind creating beautiful bursts of color. What I didn't know was that my love for plants and nature was going to follow me through to adulthood.

Living in a small house with a limited garden, I set out to try and work with nature in my home by starting my own indoor plant collection. I began with just three: *Scindapsus pictus* (satin silver pothos), *Dischidia nummularia* (string of nickels), and the gorgeous *Aeschynanthus japhrolepsis* (lipstick plant). These plants set me on my indoor plant journey.

I very quickly learned that, given the right conditions, it is indeed possible to grow and nurture just about any type of plant indoors. My passion and fascination continued to grow and quite quickly three plants had turned into fifty-five, with each and every one thriving, growing, and giving back in so many glorious ways. My indoor garden oasis was born. I had created a little pocket of plant heaven and brought the outside in, and somehow encapsulated the feel, smell, and essence of a tropical rain forest in my very own living space.

With limited room I found that having some of my plants hanging, clustered on shelving, or on a ladder shelf—thereby creating a vertical garden—would allow me to save space and expand my collection. On top of this, I started using spotlights and mirrors to reflect more light around my plants so they had 360 degrees of even light. Adding the mirrors also created an illusion of having an extra window—another light source coming into the room.

We all should incorporate nature into our lives in one way or another, and what better way to start than by inviting nature into our indoor spaces? We all have green fingers—we just need to tap into them! With my user-friendly and practical book, you can easily navigate your way through indoor plant care and successfully achieve a thriving indoor garden, bringing calm and tranquillity into your life.

My Golden Rules for Starting an Indoor Garden

When I first went plant shopping I was overwhelmed by the whole experience. I realized that I had not really thought about how plants were going to fit into my house. Just going out and randomly coming home with a plant you fancy does not work. So here I have compiled some rules to help you.

1 THINK ABOUT YOUR TIME

Owning houseplants is a rewarding hobby, but a lot goes into caring for them. Think about how busy your life is. How much time do you have to water? How often do you go away? Who will care for them when you do?

2 START OFF WITH THREE PLANTS AT THE MOST

I recommend two to three to get used to their care needs and see how they work with your lifestyle.

3 CONSIDER WHERE YOUR PLANTS WILL BE

Plants require light, air, space to grow, and the right temperature. A plant that thrives in warmer conditions should not be placed in a drafty location near a window. Keep plants away from radiators and air conditioning units, which will dry them out. Think whether you want the plant at floor level or eye level. A bold statement plant would look stunning displayed on its own. Avoid having your plants squeezed between furniture. This will prevent good airflow, which is needed for growth and to prevent soil mold and fungal disease. Common diseases are gray mold, which can attack every part of the plant and resembles fuzzy gray mold; powdery mildew, where a white powder appears on the leaves; and leaf spot, where the leaves develop yellow, black, or brown spots that can spread from leaf to leaf.

OPPOSITE Two prayer plants and a Chinese evergreen (clockwise from top): *Calathea, Aglaonema, Maranta*.

LEFT *Aloe vera*: perfectly at home in a bathroom.

4   MAXIMIZE YOUR SPACE

If shelf and table space is already occupied, hanging plants in baskets may work. Use low-light plants in darker areas. Adding artificial lighting to a shelf in your living room in a dark corner might help a plant to thrive. Cluster plants together on a vertical ladder shelf. Use all the space you have available: could a table or shelf be cleared? Don't forget window ledges (as long as they are not drafty) and floors. Also remember that humidity-loving plants will do well in a bathroom with natural light.

5   CHOOSE GOOD SPECIMENS

I would recommend buying your first plant from a plant shop or garden center rather than online. Being able to see it means you can select the perfect one for you and—even better—staff will be on hand to advise you. Some labels will specify if the plant is easy care or not.

HOW TO READ A PLANT LABEL
This should cover hardiness, size, watering, feeding, and light requirements (as well as flowering period if relevant). Don't be intimidated by Latin botanical names on labels! They simply provide a unique name for each plant—unlike common names, of which there might be several for the same plant or the same name for different plants. The first word of the name is always the genus and the second the species. Here is an example of the monstera (see page 22): "Monstera" is the genus, while there are 45 species, such as *Monstera deliciosa*, *Monstera adansonii*, and *Monstera obliqua*.

BRIGHT LIGHT
These plants must receive strong sunlight for the majority of the day. Bright light conditions can be also be created using grow lights.

MEDIUM LIGHT
Best for east- or west-facing windows that receive filtered or indirect sunlight.

LOW LIGHT
Many plants will thrive in areas with minimal light. However, low light does not mean no light! A north-facing window or a landing where the lighting is mostly fluorescent would be perfect.

INSPECT BEFORE BUYING
Avoid plants with leaf discoloration, holes in leaves, etc. Check under the leaves for any pests or pest eggs. If the plant is not too tight in the pot, gently take it out and check if its roots are healthy. Healthy roots should be white or tan and appear succulent (unless they are very fine). If roots are brown and crumbly, the plant is unhealthy. Where possible, avoid any plant with roots growing through the pot or circling around the container: it will need repotting. If there are multiples of the same plant to choose from, compare them and choose the one in best condition. Look for new growth and how many stems the plant has. I love to see new growth on a plant I am about to purchase—a sign that it is healthy.

OPPOSITE Make your own vertical garden by getting creative with shelving; ideal for small indoor spaces.

6 CONSIDER SIZE

Think about the space you have set aside at home for your new plant. It is going to grow, so consider if it is going to outgrow that space. Also take into account that a small plant is likely to be a baby, so check how big it could potentially grow. Baby plants are also more tender and sensitive to a change in environment and movement as they establish themselves, while larger plants tend to be more mature and hardier. A slow grower is so much more convenient than a fast one that will get too large for its space.

7 SELECT THE RIGHT POT

A new plant might have been in its nursery pot for some time. It may have even outgrown it to the point that it is rootbound and will need repotting once you bring it home. If so, buy a pot 2" (5cm) larger than the existing one. You can tell a plant is rootbound when you cannot pull it out of its pot. This is because all of the roots have grown and tangled themselves around the drainage holes and attached themselves to the pot. If this happens, you may have to cut up the nursery pot to free the plant.

All indoor plants need pots with drainage holes to allow excess water to drain away. A buildup of water would lead to rotting roots. Roots need not only water but air too. Soil has air pockets that are crucial for the development of healthy roots. It's a good idea to place your plants either on a saucer that will catch the water or into a decorative outer pot. Be sure to pour away the excess water that accumulates in the saucer or outer pot so that it is not sitting in water.

If you decide to put your potted plant into a decorative outer pot, consider the fit. Remember that as your plant grows it will need repotting into a slightly larger nursery pot, which will also mean you need a larger decorative pot.

OPPOSITE (From top) Heartleaf philodendron, *Begonia maculata* (polka dot begonia), *Aphelandra squarrosa* (zebra plant).

ABOVE *Chamaedorea elegans* (parlor palm).

HOUSEPLANT TOOLS

When starting your indoor garden, think about the tools and equipment you will need. These items are inexpensive and are the key things you will need when caring for your indoor plants.

- Pots
- Misting spray bottle
- Small watering can
- Large and miniature trowels
- Pruning shears
- Moisture meter
- Long-handled scissors

CHAPTER 1

REALLY EASY INDOOR PLANTS

If you are a new plant parent and are on the lookout for plants, the ones in this chapter are definitely ideal for you to start with. They are readily available in plant shops, and as they have simple care needs you could always start off with two or three. Besides being really easy to care for, what I love most about them is how simple they are to propagate. Propagating plants is always so rewarding. You can share them with friends and family or try plant swaps—something that I love to do.

Monstera adansonii (monkey mask)

COLEUS

Native to Indonesia, coleus is a tropical evergreen ornamental member of the mint family. Coleus plants have some of the most stunning colored foliage in combinations of pink, red, and maroon. Their translucent vibrant stems, together with the brightly colored leaves, really do make this plant an eye-catcher. Although coleus is normally grown outside as an annual, its vibrant foliage provides many months of gorgeous color indoors.

Coleus is easy indoors and can successfully be grown in a pot. It has a wide range of leaf sizes and can grow large or be kept small, so no matter where you are looking to place your coleus, you will be able to find one that is the perfect size. It is a great plant to brighten up any area within the home.

QUICK CARE TIPS

- Position in bright indirect light.
- Keep the coleus in slightly moist soil.
- Do not allow the soil to completely dry out.
- Cut off any buds and blooms to preserve plant energy.
- Trim off leggy stems to keep a nice shape and promote more growth.

TOP TIP Don't throw away the leggy stem trimmings. These can be popped in a glass of water and propagated to make more plants.

POSITION

Coleus thrives in bright indirect light. Do be careful not to expose it to direct sunlight as this can bleach the leaves and cause them to fade and lose color. If the plant drops its leaves, try moving it to a different location.

WATERING

When watering, keep the soil slightly moist. I prefer to water mine from the bottom—that way I can be sure the plant is taking as much water as it needs. The key to success when watering coleus is neither to saturate the soil nor to allow it to dry out completely. Slightly moist soil will keep your coleus happy and healthy.

SOIL MIX

When choosing the right soil for this plant, be sure to use a well-draining potting soil and a pot with good drainage holes. The best combination is 70 percent potting compost with 20 percent perlite and 10 percent sphagnum moss. (Perlite may look like bits of polystyrene, but it is actually a natural volcanic material that is very useful for improving both drainage and water absorption. Vermiculite, grit, and coarse sand have similar properties and can be used instead.) This mix is light in weight, and the perlite creates air pockets, preventing it from getting too compact and heavy, which could suffocate the delicate coleus roots.

Sphagnum peat moss and sphagnum moss are two different things and should not be confused. Sphagnum peat moss is the unsustainable one out of the two, because to harvest it peat bogs have to be dug up to get to the peat moss that is buried underground. Sphagnum moss, in contrast, grows on the surface and does not disturb the ground when harvested; it is able to grow back until harvested again. Read compost labels carefully to ensure the products are peat-free,

thus making them environmentally friendly and sustainable. When buying sphagnum moss always read the label to ensure that what you are buying is sourced from sustainable renewable resources.

FEEDING

Plants with colorful foliage like this need regular feeding. To help your coleus thrive, give it a dilutable liquid fertilizer every other watering during the growing season. For example, if you water every Sunday, feed it every other Sunday during the growing season. Dilute to half the strength suggested on the product label.

When using fertilizer this often, I always recommend diluting to half the strength—that way you can be sure the plant is getting what it needs but is not being overfed, which can be damaging. Underfeeding is always safer than overfeeding!

Coleus can at times grow quite leggy, so pinch the tips frequently to keep it in the shape you desire. This will also encourage your plant to grow fuller.

If given perfect conditions, in time it will start to flower, creating long purple blooms that are pretty insignificant. I would suggest cutting off the buds and flowers to preserve plant energy.

HUMIDITY

Coleus prefers medium humidity levels. Lightly mist your plant a few times a week to keep it looking lush.

PESTS

Common pests are aphids, spider mites, and mealybugs. To get rid of them, take the plant outside and blast it with a strong stream of water, making sure to hit the undersides of the leaves. This should knock off the pests. Alternatively, you can dip a cotton swab in rubbing alcohol and wipe the bugs away.

How to Propagate *Coleus*

A fast grower, in no time you will be able to propagate it. There are two simple ways to do this: a stem cutting in water or a stem cutting into soil.

1 WATER PROPAGATION

Choose a healthy stem and cut the stem to a length of around 6" (15cm).

Remove the leaves that are closest to the cut end, ensuring you keep the leaves at the top of the cutting.

Place the cutting in a glass of water and keep in bright indirect light.

Change the water every 3 days.

In approximately 10–14 days roots will have formed.

Once roots are established, you can transfer your cutting into potting soil.

OPPOSITE Here a mature coleus plant has started to flower, showing its long delicate violet blooms.

NODES

A node is the part of a stem where buds are located and it appears as a raised area. If you cut the stem just above a node, new growth will start from there, while cutting just below a node encourages roots to form. (Internodes are the sections of stem between the nodes and are the vessels that carry water and nutrients from node to node.) When pruning or taking cuttings for propagation, it is important to locate the node.

2 SOIL PROPAGATION

Choose a healthy stem for your cutting and cut the stem below the third node down (see above).

Snip off the lowest leaves at the end of the stem cutting.

Dip the cut end in hormone rooting powder (see box opposite).

Gently push down the stem cutting into the soil (submerging two nodes).

Repeat the same process with all of the stem cuttings.

Lightly water the soil and the cuttings.

Keep in bright indirect light. After approximately 4 weeks, roots will have formed and new growth will start to sprout from the cuttings.

HORMONE ROOTING POWDER

Hormone rooting powder stimulates root formation and often contains a fungicide to prevent rot while the cutting creates new roots. Some plants are more difficult to propagate than others, and rooting hormone increases your chances of success.

MONSTERA DELICIOSA (SWISS CHEESE PLANT)

Native to the tropical rain forest from southern Mexico to Panama, the fabulous *Monstera deliciosa* is famous for its natural perforated holes—hence the nickname Swiss cheese plant.

In the wild it grows enormous and indoors can spread up to 24" (60cm) wide. Swiss cheese plants are very easy to care for, so with minimal attention you can successfully grow it in the home or office. They do need a lot of space, however. Having one in a statement pot displayed on its own in an open space will surely deliver.

In the wild, the plant attaches itself to trees and is a natural climber. When grown indoors under the right conditions, it can increase in height by up to 24" (60cm) per year. It naturally wants to grow wide but can be trained to climb up a moss pole for convenience. To maintain its desired size, I would suggest that you avoid repotting too often.

Do consider whether the space you have in the home or office is suitable. Because these monstrous plants can grow huge, it's a good idea to prune them. They are also very easy to propagate. Cutting just below the node (the point where the leaves emerge from the stem), place in water and after 2–3 weeks roots will have formed. The famous Swiss cheese plant is definitely worth owning as it's very easy to look after and is stunning as a feature plant in any space.

POSITION

It thrives in medium to bright indirect light. While the plant is also tolerant of lower light conditions, low light will make it grow too leggy. Removing dust from the leaves with a damp cloth will also help the leaves to absorb light.

WATERING

Water every 1–2 weeks, allowing the soil to dry out in between watering. You may need to water more frequently in the summer months and less in the winter. If the leaf tips turn brown, you are either watering inconsistently or overfeeding, which causes the leaf edges to burn.

SOIL MIX

It requires rich, nutrient-dense soil that holds moisture but doesn't remain soggy.

Use a regular potting soil mixed equally with coco coir.

FEEDING

Feed once a month during the spring and summer using a dilutable fertilizer. Dilute to half the strength recommended on the product label.

HUMIDITY

Monstera deliciosa enjoys a humid environment. Misting the leaves frequently to increase the humidity around the plant is sufficient.

PESTS

The common pests are thrips, scale insects, spider mites, and fungus gnats. Check the soil and the underside of leaves often to ensure there is no infestation. A neem oil solution can be sprayed over the entire plant to get rid of pests.

MONSTERA ADANSONII (MONKEY MASK)

A smaller relative to the Swiss cheese plant, *Monstera adansonii* has become popular among houseplant enthusiasts. Native to South and Central America, this is one of the easiest indoor plants to care for, making it a go-to plant for new plant parents. As the plant matures, its heart-shaped leaves develop holes that resemble Swiss cheese (this process is called fenestration). Because of the leaf appearance, it is commonly known as the "monkey mask" plant. I love how versatile this plant is to have displayed in the home. With its vining abilities *Monstera adansonii* will thrive on a shelf, hanging in a basket, or attached to a moss pole, making it easy to find the perfect location within the home or office. *Monstera adansonii* is a fast grower but will remain manageable when grown in a container indoors. Regular pruning will help keep the plant to the desired size. With simple care, it will thrive and bring a tropical vibe to any indoor space.

QUICK CARE TIPS

- Keep in bright indirect light.
- Thrives in evenly moist soil.
- Increase humidity with frequent misting, a pebble tray, or humidifier.
- Check under leaves for scale insects or spider mites.
- Because *Monstera adansonii* is a fast grower, you will need to trim it back at times. Don't waste the cuttings! It can easily be propagated in water. Because it has aerial roots, this makes water propagation even easier. Simply take your cuttings and place them in water. Position in bright indirect light and within two weeks roots will develop. Once roots have established, the cuttings can be put in soil. See pages 60–62 for more detail on how to propagate plants with aerial roots.

    Propagating plants is always so rewarding. Whether you choose to create a fuller plant or grow a new one, the best part of propagating for me is sharing my plants with others.

POSITION

In its habitat *Monstera adansonii* grows in partial shade under large trees in the jungle, with very little direct-sun exposure. Mimicking these light conditions indoors will protect the leaves from sun scorch. Position it in bright indirect light.

WATERING

Monstera thrives in evenly moist soil. When the top 4" (10cm) of soil are dry, then give the plant a drink, ensuring any excess water drains out of the drainage holes. During the warmer summer months, water once a week; water every two weeks in the cooler months.

SOIL MIX

When repotting, the best soil is a regular potting mix that contains coco coir. Coco coir added to potting media increases moisture retention without the soil becoming waterlogged and increases aeration around the roots.

FEEDING

Feed once a month during the growing season with a dilutable plant fertilizer. Dilute to the recommended ratio on the product label. During the winter months there is no need to feed as the plant is not growing as much.

HUMIDITY

Monstera adansonii loves humidity. After all, it is native to tropical rain forests and jungles, which are naturally damp. Humidity can be increased around your plants in the home by using a pebble tray, humidifier, or frequent misting.

PESTS

The two most common pests to look out for are scale insects and spider mites. Check under the leaves often to ensure no infestation has developed. Scale can be removed by using a cotton swab dipped in rubbing alcohol. For spider mites or a larger population of scale, I recommend using organic neem oil.

PILEA PEPEROMIOIDES (CHINESE MONEY PLANT)

The Chinese money plant is definitely one of my favorite easy indoor plants. Native to the Yunnan and Sichuan provinces in southern China, this unusual-looking plant is a must-have when starting your indoor garden. Chinese money plants are relatively small, growing to a height of 8"–12" (20–30cm), so these gorgeous babies do well in pots. Their saucer-shaped leaves are what make them really stand out; they grow to approximately 4" (10cm).

Relatively low maintenance and with the added bonus of air-purifying qualities and easy propagation, what's not to love? So if you're starting your plant journey or wanting to add to your existing indoor garden, here are some care tips.

QUICK CARE TIPS

- Rotate the plant 90 degrees every few weeks so that it does not bend toward the light.
- Keep the surface of the leaves dust free so that they can easily absorb the light the plant needs.
- Lightly mist every few days to prevent the leaf edges from turning crispy.
- The best time to repot is in spring/summer. This is the plant's active season so roots will need a larger pot to grow. You will also notice tiny offshoots from your plant—these are commonly known as "pups." Pups are new baby money plants growing. A healthy mature plant will produce many pups that can be propagated easily.
- Propagation is done by separating the pups from the rhizome or stem of the parent plant. (Rhizomes are underground horizontal plant stems able to send out roots and shoots of a new plant.) These can be placed in water or planted directly into soil. Putting your plantlets in bright indirect light and lightly moist conditions will help them to establish roots and thrive.

POSITION

It thrives in bright indirect light. Do not place in direct sunlight as this will burn the leaves. A bit of light shade will encourage larger leaves. Keeping the surface of the leaves dust free will also help the plant to absorb the light it needs.

WATERING

Allow the soil to dry out in between watering to prevent saturated roots and root rot. During the winter months, feel free to only water once every two weeks. Lightly misting the plant will keep it happy too, preventing crispy leaf edges.

If you notice the young leaves turning yellow or falling off, it's likely that the plant has been overwatered. A point to remember is that older leaves will naturally turn yellow and drop off, so if you have been watering your plant correctly, natural old leaf drop is part of the plant's life cycle and you have nothing to worry about.

SOIL MIX

It requires well-draining potting soil and, as with all indoor plants, a pot with good drainage holes. I like to add perlite to my potting mix for extra aeration and to aid drainage.

FEEDING

Once a month, feed with an all-purpose plant fertilizer to keep the nutrient levels up. During the winter months you can cut back on feeding. Soft leaves are a sign of too much fertilizer.

HUMIDITY

Chinese money plants enjoy medium humidity levels. Increase the humidity by spritzing the plant several times a week with water. You can tell the humidity is too low if the plant develops brown patches on the tips or sides of its leaves.

PESTS

Common pests are aphids, spider mites, mealybugs, and scale insects. To get rid of pests, simply use a cotton swab dipped in rubbing alcohol and wipe them off, paying particular attention to the undersides of the leaves.

DRACAENA MARGINATA (DRAGON TREE)

Native to Mauritius and Madagascar, the dragon tree has long striking leaves with red edges and looks stunning on its own or placed among other plants to create height. Taller varieties will look great in a large pot displayed as a floor plant.

I love the aesthetics of the dragon tree—the plant has a tropical look about it, almost mimicking palm trees, so bringing one of them home will definitely add a unique feel to your indoor space.

The dragon tree is low maintenance and can last for years. A great feature plant for any indoor space, this stunning evergreen tree can reach heights of around 6 feet (1.8m) indoors. However, it is a very slow grower so will take years to get there.

QUICK CARE TIPS

- Position in bright indirect light, never direct sunlight.
- Wipe the leaves with a damp cloth to keep them dust free.
- Mist the plant to raise the humidity and promote lush healthy leaves.
- Look out for brown leaf tips and edges, a clear sign of underwatering or not enough humidity.
- Numerous yellow leaves are an indication of overwatering. However, if older leaves start turning yellow and crispy, do not worry. This plant is similar to the yucca: the oldest leaves will always die back first to allow for new growth. Cut off any dead leaves, cutting back closest to the trunk (cane).

POSITION

The dragon tree thrives best in medium indirect sunlight but can tolerate low light situations. Be sure not to place it in direct sunlight. Pale bleached leaves indicate that the plant is getting too much light. Look out for consistent small leaf growth: a clear indication that the plant isn't getting enough light.

WATERING

The dragon tree does not require a lot of water and is happiest when the soil is kept moist but not soggy. Water about once a week or every other week, allowing the soil to dry out between watering. Use a pot with good drainage holes to allow any excess water to drain away and prevent roots from suffocating.

SOIL MIX

The dragon tree requires well-draining soil. You can create your own mix by combining 50 percent regular potting soil with 50 percent perlite.

FEEDING

It is a slow grower so does not require too much fertilizer. Feed once a month in the spring and summer months with a liquid all-purpose plant food.

HUMIDITY

It will do well in the average indoor environment. However, regular misting will benefit the plant, keeping the leaves looking lush and healthy. Keep away from drafts as well as excessive central heating as this will dry out the leaves.

PESTS

While pests are not common, you may find scale insects and mealybugs. To get rid of them, simply use a cotton swab with rubbing alcohol and wipe them away. Alternatively, shower the whole plant with a strong stream of water. With large varieties, the easiest way is to put the plant in the bath and shower over the foliage until all pests are removed.

- Prune old leaves to encourage new growth.
- Position in bright indirect light.
- Water when the top inch of soil is dry.
- Frequent misting will increase humidity around the plant.
- Check under leaves and on stems for pests.

PACHIRA AQUATICA (GUIANA CHESTNUT)

Pachira aquatica, more commonly known as the Guiana chestnut, is a wetland tree native to Central and South America where it will be found growing in swamps. This fascinating plant, which is seen potted with twisted braided trunks, has become an attractive houseplant thanks to its hardy nature. However, it does not grow like this in the wild. It has become a tradition to weave the trunks together to create a classic tree shape.

If you're exploring the idea of having an indoor tree in the home but don't know where to begin, the Guiana chestnut is the one to go for. You can have it grow as large or as little as you want. It's also known as the money tree and it's thought that having one in the home brings good luck; for those practising feng shui it is believed to bring positive "chi" or energy into the home. Besides being an easy indoor plant, the enchanting beliefs that come with it have made it a popular choice. I have the Guiana chestnut in my own indoor garden. Because they are naturally found in swamps, they are forgiving if accidently overwatered, which is a common mistake.

Money trees are large plants, so do think about the best place to put yours. When grown in a container it can reach to a height of 6 feet (1.8m). This is not the type of plant that can be popped on a shelf! It needs a well-thought-out space that will cope with the height, and with the added leaf spread resembling a canopy it will need elbow room as well. The great news is that it is not toxic to humans or pets, which makes it a lot easier to find the perfect location to display. This plant is best placed on a side table by itself or on the floor.

Prune the leaves throughout the year to encourage new leaf growth. Repotting once every 1–2 years into a slightly larger pot will encourage it to keep growing.

POSITION

Money trees require bright indirect light for at least six hours a day. They will also do well under fluorescent light.

WATERING

Water regularly. When the top inch of soil is dry, it is time to water. During the spring and summer months, the plant will require more frequent watering. During the winter, water less often.

SOIL MIX

Whether you're repotting or just changing the soil, use a regular potting soil mixed with coarse sand and added perlite.

FEEDING

To keep the feeding routine easy with this plant in particular, go by this guide. Feed every four waters during the growing season and every six waters in the winter months. Use an organic, dilutable plant fertilizer at the strength recommended on the product label during the growing season and half that strength during the winter.

HUMIDITY

The money tree does appreciate higher humidity levels. Frequent misting, adding a humidifier, or a pebble tray will benefit the plant. Placing in the bathroom is always a good option too if the light conditions are right.

PESTS

Common pests that are attracted to the money tree are mealybugs and scale insects. Check under the leaves and on stems regularly. If pests are present, mist the whole plant with an organic neem oil solution.

SCHEFFLERA (UMBRELLA PLANT)

Schefflera is so stunning to look at, making this one of my favorite easy indoor plants. I have one in my collection. Native to Australia and surrounding countries, its leaf formations resemble umbrellas, giving the plant its common name. Schefflera plants come in many different varieties. *Schefflera arboricola*, known as the dwarf umbrella tree, can grow to a mature height of 36"–48" (90–125cm) indoors. One of the reasons it is popular is because the plant is so easy to care for. However, it is toxic to both people and animals, so do bear this in mind when finding a suitable location in the home.

Schefflera plants are slow when grown in containers indoors, which means they won't require repotting often. The main reasons to repot any plant would be to allow it to grow bigger or replace depleted soil. Keep in mind when repotting that it is a dwarf tree and it will grow taller in a larger pot. If you wish to keep it the same size, I would suggest removing it from the pot, gently trimming its roots, giving the plant fresh soil, and putting it back in the same pot. The best time to do any repotting is in spring.

POSITION
Schefflera thrives in bright indirect light. If you notice the plant becoming leggy and floppy, this is an indication that it is not getting enough light.

WATERING
Water once the soil is almost completely dried out. Do not water if the top half is still moist.

SOIL MIX
Schefflera will grow at its best in a well-drained, sandy potting mix. Using a regular potting soil with added coarse sand or perlite to improve drainage would be sufficient.

FEEDING
During the growing season, feed once a month with a soluble plant fertilizer diluted to the strength recommended.

HUMIDITY
It will appreciate frequent misting; this will increase leaf quality and prevent the leaves from drying up. Placing the plant on a pebble tray will also help to raise the humidity.

PESTS
Aphids, mealybugs, spider mites, and scale insects are the common pests attracted to schefflera. Check often to ensure no infestation has developed. If pests are present, mist the whole plant with an organic neem oil solution.

YUCCA

Another favorite, the yucca is definitely the go-to plant for new plant parents. It's very easy to find and has become a popular houseplant. Growing yucca in pots indoors is a fabulous way to bring the outdoors inside in a large way, adding a focal point to the room.

Native to the Caribbean, the high deserts of the southwestern United States, and Mexico, yucca plants are striking and low maintenance. They are slow so will not outgrow their pot quickly and will not need repotting for many years. Also, an added bonus is that they are drought tolerant, so if you forget to water or go away for a short break they will be fine. They are relatively inexpensive and often come in a large pot, perfect for displaying as a floor plant.

POSITION
Your yucca will thrive in full sunlight. Placing it in the brightest location indoors is the best position. Near a south-, east-, or west-facing window would be perfect.

WATERING
Yucca plants are prone to overwatering. Be mindful when watering as they do not like to sit in water. Always use a pot with good drainage holes. Water regularly in the summer months, allowing the soil to dry out between watering. Water once every few weeks in the winter months. It's better to underwater rather than overwater.

SOIL MIX
Native to hot climates, yuccas grow in sandy soil, so the main requirement is a well-draining mix. When repotting, use a regular potting compost and mix with coarse sand and perlite to help with drainage. Yucca plants do not require a highly fertile soil.

QUICK CARE TIPS

- Lower leaves will always droop and die back first. Trim any yellow, crispy dead leaves back to near the trunk.
- Do not overwater or allow the yucca to sit in water.
- Place in the brightest lit area in the home.
- Use a sturdy ceramic or terracotta pot. The canes do get heavy, so this will give it a solid base to ensure it doesn't topple over.
- Mildly toxic to cats and dogs.

FEEDING
Feed once a month during the growing season. Use a liquid fertilizer and dilute to half the strength recommended on the product label. An overfed yucca can result in leaf burn; using half-strength fertilizer helps prevent salt and mineral buildup in the soil.

HUMIDITY
Yuccas are adaptable to the ever-changing indoor environment. However, misting during the winter months when the central heating is likely to be on (causing dry air) will help prevent browning leaf edges.

PESTS
Common pests are aphids, mealybugs, and scale insects. To get rid of them, simply shower the whole plant with a strong stream of water (perhaps easier outside or in the bath); once dry, spray it with an organic neem oil solution. Pay attention to the undersides of the leaves too!

ZAMIOCULCAS ZAMIIFOLIA (ZZ PLANT)

Zamioculcas zamiifolia has a mouthful of a botanical name. More commonly known as the ZZ (pronounced Zee-Zee) plant, it is striking to look at. Native to dry grasslands and forests in eastern Africa, it has become a popular indoor plant and luckily for us is easy to find in plant shops and garden centers. The ZZ plant has very distinctive dark green, glossy leaves, indicating that it absorbs light even from minimal sources. It is a very low-maintenance indoor plant that tolerates neglect, so if you miss a watering or two it will be forgiving. It is definitely a great choice for beginners who would like to own a plant that isn't demanding. Another positive point to raise about the ZZ plant is that it is good to have in your collection if you have a busy lifestyle or often go away on vacation.

ZZ plants are slow growers. When mature they can reach 36" (90cm) high. This means your plant will not outgrow its container quickly. Repotting every two years to a pot that is one size larger than the one it previously lived in is all that is required, adding to its convenience.

As well as being an easy indoor plant, it is also an air purifier, making it great to have at home and in office environments.

POSITION

The ZZ plant is quite forgiving when it comes to light conditions. It prefers medium to bright indirect light, but it is extremely adaptable. It will tolerate low light conditions, including fluorescent lighting in a windowless location.

WATERING

Although it is drought tolerant, this does not mean no water! A good rule of thumb is to allow the soil to completely dry out. When watering, ensure the soil is saturated enough that the water drains out of the pot drainage holes—that way you can be sure the roots have had a good drink before the next watering. Note that the ZZ plant does not like to sit in wet soil.

SOIL MIX

It will only need repotting every two years. The perfect combination is regular potting soil mixed with perlite and cactus compost to improve aeration.

FEEDING

Feed once a month in the growing season from spring to autumn with an organic dilutable fertilizer. Dilute to half the strength recommended on the product label; if it is too strong, the fertilizer can damage the plant's foliage and root system.

HUMIDITY

It is hardy so will thrive in average room environments.

PESTS

Aphids, mites, whiteflies, scale insects, mealybugs, and gnats are common bugs attracted to the ZZ plant. Keep it in a well-ventilated area and check regularly for any signs of pests. If they are found, spray with a neem oil solution.

- Water when soil is completely dry.
- Repot every two years.
- Check leaves for any pests.
- Propagate by cutting off a stalk at the base of the plant. Put the cut stem in water (change the water every two weeks); place in bright indirect light, and roots will develop.

Pachira aquatica is also known as the Guiana chestnut or money tree. It has become an attractive houseplant thanks to its hardy nature.

OPPOSITE *Dracaena marginata*, commonly known as the dragon tree, brings a tropical vibe to any indoor space.

WHAT YOU NEED TO REMEMBER ABOUT REALLY EASY PLANTS

- Use pots with good drainage holes.
- If you are prone to overwatering, use a moisture reader.
- Snip off any yellow or dead leaves to encourage new growth.
- Because the plants in this category are "easy," they don't need as much attention as, for example, a "diva." But check often for pests. Bugs left unchecked will spread to your other indoor plants.
- Dusty leaves makes it harder for your plants to absorb the light. Keep leaves dust free by giving them a wipe with a wet cloth once a week.
- Easy indoor plants tend to reward you with a lot of fast growth—they may even outgrow their place quickly. Prune your plant back into shape and use what you have removed as cuttings to increase your collection or give away.

CHAPTER 2

AIR-PURIFYING PLANTS

Bringing specific plants into homes and office spaces can have the added benefit of purifying the air. Through photosynthesis, plants convert the carbon dioxide we exhale into fresh oxygen, and they can also remove toxins from the air we breathe. The plants in this chapter are the champions when it comes to purifying the air. There are many to choose from here, making it easier to find the perfect air-purifying plant to bring inside your living/work spaces.

Nephrolepis exaltata (Boston fern)

NEPHROLEPIS EXALTATA (BOSTON FERN)

Introducing you to one of my favorite indoor ferns: the Boston fern. Native to North America, it has grown in popularity as an indoor plant. Not only is the Boston fern lush and beautiful, it turns out that ferns are the best plants for removing indoor pollutants, so having it in the home or office will give you the added benefit of purifying the air.

Boston ferns come in different sizes. Smaller ferns look great displayed on a shelf or side table clustered among other humidity-loving plants, while larger, fuller ones look stunning in a hanging basket. Hanging baskets for larger ferns are always a great idea so they have the space around them to stretch and unfurl new frond growth. Large ferns also look less intimidating when hanging (see picture on page 11).

(see picture on page 11)

QUICK CARE TIPS

- Position in bright indirect light. Do not expose to direct sunlight.
- Keep the soil moist but not soaking wet.
- Keep the humidity level high: display in the bathroom, mist daily or add a humidifier.
- Display larger Boston ferns in a hanging basket.

Look out for:

Browning fronds and leaf edges, which may be caused by lack of light, not enough humidity, underwatering or too much light. Assess the lighting conditions and your routine to identify which care need has been neglected.

Learning how to take care of Boston ferns is not difficult; however, they do have specific requirements to keep your fern happy and beautiful. They thrive in cool, humid environments, so be sure to meet its humidity needs. Winter can be a tricky time when heating is on in the home, so provide it with the extra humidity it needs by frequent misting or adding a humidifier nearby. It's a good idea to soak the whole plant and pot once a month to keep it fully hydrated, making sure all excess water drains away.

Following these care guidelines will help you to grow the Boston fern indoors successfully.

POSITION

Boston ferns are pretty adaptable but thrive best in medium and bright indirect light conditions. Do not expose to direct sunlight as this will burn and scorch the leaves.

WATERING

They need moist soil at all times but not soaking wet. During the winter season allow the top 2" (5cm) of soil to slightly dry out in between watering.

SOIL MIX

Boston ferns thrive in light, airy soil. Adding perlite to the mix will improve airflow around the roots and ensure proper drainage after watering.

FEEDING

Feed with a dilutable liquid fertilizer once a month during the spring and summer months. Dilute as recommended on the product label.

HUMIDITY

The more humidity you can provide this plant the better. Displaying in the bathroom if possible is always the easiest option. Misting daily is a must, or place near a humidifier. Keep the plant away from heaters and air vents to prevent dehydration.

PESTS

Common pests are mealybugs, scale insects, and spider mites. The simplest way to eradicate pests is to drench and spray the whole plant, particularly under the leaf fronds, with an organic neem oil solution.

QUICK CARE TIPS

- Place in bright indirect light.
- Allow soil to slightly dry out in between watering. Do not allow roots to sit in water.
- Keep humidity levels high around the plant with frequent misting or add a humidifier.
- Look out for pests by checking under the leaves and blooms.
- Toxic to humans and pets.

ANTHURIUM ANDRAEANUM (FLAMINGO LILY)

Native to the West Indies, Colombia, and Ecuador, the stunning *Anthurium andraeanum* is not only relatively easy but also has the added benefit of being an air-purifying plant. Placing it in the home or office is a great way to clean the air naturally.

Most commonly called the flamingo lily or painter's palette, it is a beautiful evergreen easily recognizable by its gorgeous waxy flowers. I particularly love this plant for the lush green leaves and striking red flower display.

Displaying it in the home on a simple shelf, on the office desk, or a side table will most certainly add a vibrant pop of color to any indoor space. Its eye-catching look can be achieved all year round when its needs are met, and it is a great choice for any plant lover. Note, however, that anthuriums are toxic to humans and pets if ingested.

To successfully grow indoors it's a good idea to try and imitate the rain forest conditions as much as you can. It thrives in humid environments, so don't rule out displaying this beauty in the bathroom or clustered among other humidity-loving plants. I have even seen it in hairdressers' enjoying the salon air.

POSITION

In the rain forest, the flamingo lily grows on lower ground. Not much direct light reaches the level under the canopy of trees, so position it in bright indirect light. If placing near a window, avoid direct sunlight as this will burn and scorch the leaves. On the other hand, if the lighting conditions are too low, the plant will not produce blooms.

WATERING

Flamingo lilies like medium moisture. Allow the soil to dry out a little in between watering. Ensure excess water drains out of the pot drainage holes as they do not like to sit in water. Yellow young leaves are a sign of overwatering.

SOIL MIX

The best soil mixture is equal parts of coco coir, regular potting soil, and perlite.

FEEDING

To keep your plant lush and flowering, feed every 3 weeks during the spring and summer months with a dilutable fertilizer. Dilute to half the strength recommended on the product label.

HUMIDITY

The flamingo lily thrives in humidity levels of 80 percent or above. Keeping it in a brightly lit kitchen or bathroom is an easy way to give the plant what it needs. Alternatively, mist daily or place on a pebble tray or near a humidifier. Ensure you spray the aerial roots too. These are roots that can grow above the soil.

PESTS

The most common pests are mealybugs, aphids, thrips, scale insects, and spider mites, which are more likely to infest this plant in the warm summer months. Do look out for any signs by checking under the leaves and under the blooms. The best method for getting rid of all of these pests is by using an organic neem oil spray mixture. Simply spray the whole plant, especially under the leaves, rinse, and spray over again.

SPATHIPHYLLUM (PEACE LILY)

Spathiphyllum, commonly known as the peace lily, is native to the tropical rain forest of Colombia and Venezuela. Not only is it a stunningly elegant plant, but also it absorbs pollutants from the air through the leaves, sending them to the roots where the chemicals are broken down by microbes in the soil. We can all benefit from this beautiful plant's air-purifying qualities by growing it in our homes and offices. Peace lily is easy to care for and often forgiving of neglect.

If you want an easy indoor flowering plant with attractive foliage and white blooms, this is definitely one to go for. It is a moderate grower, which means it will not need repotting more than once a year in the spring with fresh soil. This also means it will not outgrow its space quickly in the home. Move into a larger pot when roots have completely outgrown the container.

Peace lilies come in different sizes. Tall plants look great in a large floor pot, while smaller varieties look stunning displayed alone to show off their elegance or on shelving.

POSITION
They like bright indirect light from a nearby window. They will not bloom in low light conditions and will also grow too leggy if sufficient light is not provided. Be sure that the plant is not in direct sunlight.

WATERING
Keep the soil consistently moist but not soaking wet. They do not like to sit in water. Ensure excess water drains out of the pot drainage holes to prevent soaking roots, which will lead to root rot.

SOIL MIX
Use a potting soil mixed with perlite, coco coir, and a cactus compost to create a well-draining, lightweight growing medium.

FEEDING
Peace lilies do not require frequent feeding. To promote growth in the spring and summer months, feed every 6 weeks starting in late winter using a dilutable liquid fertilizer. Dilute as recommended on the product label.

HUMIDITY
Being tropical plants, they require humidity levels of around 50 percent. To increase the humidity, mist daily or place near a humidifier or on a pebble tray. Browning leaf edges are a sign the plant is not getting enough humidity.

PESTS
The three most common pests are aphids, mealybugs, and spider mites. Spraying the plant and under leaves with an organic neem oil solution will get rid of them. Checking under the leaves often to ensure no pests have infested the plant is always a good idea.

QUICK CARE TIPS

- Keep in medium indirect light.
- Mist the leaves every so often. Remember, frequent misting will encourage larger leaf growth.
- Trimming the plant at the node (where the leaves emerge from the stem) will encourage it to grow bushier.
- Cuttings from the plant can easily be propagated in water.
- Check under the leaves for any sign of pests.

PHILODENDRON HEDERACEUM (HEARTLEAF PHILODENDRON)

Native to the West Indies, Mexico, and Brazil, the beautiful heartleaf philodendron is an easy plant to recognize due to its distinctive glossy heart-shaped leaves. Heartleaf philodendrons are not only extremely easy to care for but also have the ability to remove toxins from the air indoors, making them a fantastic choice in the home and office.

The elegant heartleaf philodendron is a trailing plant so it will look stunning displayed on the corner of a bookshelf or hanging in a basket; alternatively, you can train it to climb a moss pole as it loves to grow upward too! Generally, heartleaf philodendrons come in many different sizes, which make it easier to find the perfect location.

Despite being native to tropical environments, it is tolerant of dry air although it will appreciate being misted every so often.

To keep the plant to the desired shape and length or to create a fuller plant, trim the stems just under a node (where the leaves emerge from the stem). New growth will occur from the node. Heartleaf philodendrons are also very easy to propagate, so if you have trimmed your plant, don't waste the cuttings! Simply pop them in water and roots will develop after a few weeks or they can be put into soil to create new plants. They can also be popped back in with the mother plant to make it bushier. See pages 60–62 for more detail on taking cuttings.

With a little care and attention, you can successfully grow the heartleaf philodendron indoors, thus bringing the joys of nature from outside into your indoor space with the added benefit of its air-purifying qualities.

POSITION

Heartleaf philodendrons thrive in medium indirect light. Do not expose to direct sunlight as this will scorch the leaves.

WATERING

Keep the soil lightly moist from spring until autumn. Allow the surface of the soil to dry out in between watering during the winter months. If you notice yellow leaves, this is a sign of overwatering.

SOIL MIX

Heartleaf philodendrons require a well-draining soil. Whether you are repotting into a larger pot or simply replenishing the soil, the best one to use is 50 percent regular potting soil mixed with 50 percent coco coir.

FEEDING

Feed with a soluble liquid fertilizer once every 3–4 weeks during the growing season. Dilute as recommended on the product label.

HUMIDITY

Heartleaf philodendrons will thrive in regular indoor environments and are tolerant of dry-air conditions. However, if you want to encourage larger leaf growth, regular misting will be required.

PESTS

Pests are not normally a problem. If they do occur, the common ones are aphids, scale insects, spider mites, or mealybugs. They can easily be eradicated by washing all of the leaves and stems with water, and spraying with an organic neem oil solution.

TRADESCANTIA ZEBRINA (SILVER INCH PLANT)

Tradescantia zebrina is also known as Zebrina or the silver inch plant. Native to Mexico, it has become a popular indoor trailing plant and is one of my favorites. You can't help but be attracted to its stunning striped leaves with metallic silver on top and deep purple underneath; purple is my favorite color, so this plant really stands out to me.

It is easy to care for, so if you're looking for an easy indoor plant with an eye-catching appearance, this is a great choice. Zebrina can be found in many different sizes, making it simple to find a perfect location indoors. It can be grown in hanging baskets to show off the trailing shimmering leaves or be kept compact in a pot. However, be aware that it can be toxic to pets and humans.

When given the right care, it is a fast grower. You may decide to let it continuously grow and trail, but to maintain the desired shape, snip the stems at the node (where the leaves emerge from the stems) to make it more manageable. To encourage new growth and keep it bushy, frequent trimming will be needed. The great news is that propagation is a cinch, so after trimming, those cuttings can easily be propagated in water. Simply take a 3" (7cm) cutting from the stem with a node at the bottom and place the cut end in water. After a week, roots will start to form.

One important factor to know is that they have a relatively short lifespan. No matter how attentive you are, eventually all the leaves will drop off and only long stems will be left. While the plant is healthy and bushy, I suggest taking many stem cuttings to propagate and start off new ones!

POSITION
Place in bright indirect light. If it is not receiving enough light, the stunning metallic leaf pattern will fade.

WATERING
Water regularly as it requires the soil to be evenly moist at all times but not soaking wet. After watering, ensure all excess water has drained out of the pot drainage holes so that the roots do not sit in water.

SOIL MIX
Use a potting mix that has equal parts of soil, perlite, and coarse sand.

FEEDING
Feed with a dilutable liquid fertilizer once a month from spring to summer. Dilute as recommended on the product label. Do not feed during autumn and winter.

HUMIDITY
Zebrina does like humidity. If it is in a hanging basket, mist a few times a week. If in a pot, placing it on a pebble tray will also increase the humidity.

PESTS
Common pests are spider mites, aphids, mealybugs, whiteflies, scale insects, and thrips. To get rid of pests, use a mixture of 1 Tbsp. (15ml) castile soap per 3 oz. (1 L) of water and spray it on the leaves.

QUICK CARE TIPS

- Place in bright indirect light. Too little light will cause the leaf pattern to fade.
- Trim to encourage it to grow bushier.
- Frequently mist the plant or place on a pebble tray to keep the humidity levels up.
- Cuttings can easily be rooted in water.
- It has a relatively short lifespan, so take cuttings to start growing a replacement.
- Toxic to humans and pets.

HEDERA HELIX (ENGLISH IVY)

Native to northern Europe, English ivy is one of the most recognizable plants. It is an elegant vining plant that grows long, so when displayed indoors it brings the outside in, adding a botanical feel to any inside space. There are many different varieties of English ivy ranging from lush deep green to variegated leaf patterns.

I particularly love its air-purifying qualities. Admired for its potential to pull harmful toxins, molds, and impurities out of the air and into the leaves and roots, English ivy is a great choice to have in any indoor space. Given the right care, it is a relatively easy plant.

Though commonly grown indoors as a hanging plant, it has aerial roots that can easily be trained to climb a moss pole or trellis. It would look stunning hanging in a basket or placed on a high shelf cascading its elegant leaves.

English ivies put out vigorous growth with lush new leaves. They also produce aerial roots that grow from the twisted stems so it can take a while to fill the pot with roots. Plants should be repotted every two years in spring to a larger pot. Regularly prune your plant to keep it to the desired length. Light pruning can be done at any time of the year, so do not be afraid to give it a little snip here and there to keep the plant manageable. Note that pruning will encourage it to grow fuller and bushier. By following these simple care guides, you can successfully grow English ivy indoors.

POSITION

It grows best in bright light but not direct sun. Ivies tolerate medium to low light conditions; however, the growth rate will be reduced and variegated varieties may turn green, losing the leaf patterns and markings.

WATERING

When watering, allow the top inch of soil to dry before watering again. Keep the soil evenly moist but not soggy. Ivies do not like to sit in water, so ensure the water drains thoroughly out of the pot drainage holes.

SOIL MIX

It prefers well-draining soil. Use a regular potting soil mixed with perlite for extra drainage.

FEEDING

It's a fast grower so topping it up with nutrients in the growing season is a must. Feed once a month in the spring and summer months with a liquid fertilizer. Dilute as recommended on the product label.

HUMIDITY

Ivies love humidity. Frequent misting or displaying the plant on a pebble tray will be sufficient to give it the humidity it requires.

PESTS

Mealybugs, aphids, whiteflies, and mites are the most common pests. Use a neem oil solution to spray the whole plant to get rid of them.

FICUS LYRATA (FIDDLE-LEAF FIG)

Ficus lyrata is commonly known as the fiddle-leaf fig. Native to western Africa from Cameroon to Sierra Leone, it naturally occurs in lowland tropical rain forests. Fiddle-leaf figs have grown in popularity as houseplants, and make a wonderful choice not only for how they look but also for their air-purifying qualities. In plant shops, they can be found in different sizes; in the wild, they can grow 40–50 feet (12–15m) tall, though indoors they will be a fraction of that size.

It is a stunning plant with huge glossy, heavily veined leaves that grows upright on a slim trunk. If you want to make a statement, this is the plant to have. The fiddle-leaf fig will most certainly be a feature in any indoor space. It is toxic to animals so be mindful where you position the plant and ensure it is out of reach of pets.

Because it is actually a tree, you may find that a smaller variety suits your home better than a large one. One thing to consider is that it is a fairly fast grower so it may outgrow its space. The fiddle-leaf fig can also be repotted at any time of the year. Larger varieties are best placed in floor pots in an area where they can be allowed to grow up to at least 6 feet (1.8m) tall.

In my experience, they are easy to care for and it doesn't take that much to keep them happy and healthy. The best starting point is to find a day of the week that is convenient for you to plan your watering schedule—"fiddle-leaf Fridays" works for me! They are native to rain forests so are used to receiving a huge deluge of water with dry spells in between.

POSITION

It thrives in bright light conditions so find the brightest location indoors. Placing the plant in a window that receives direct morning or afternoon light will keep it happy.

WATERING

Water once a week, which will allow the soil to dry out in between watering. As noted above, having a watering schedule for this plant helps. Choose a day of the week to water and stick to it.

SOIL MIX

Fiddle-leaf figs require a certain type of well-draining soil. When repotting, use a mix containing 1 part coco coir, 1 part perlite, and 2 parts regular potting soil. These ingredients are widely available and inexpensive so you could easily create this soil blend yourself.

FEEDING

Feed with a liquid fertilizer once a month from spring to autumn and every three months from autumn to spring. Dilute as recommended on the product label.

HUMIDITY

Fiddle-leaf figs thrive in humidity conditions of between 40 and 60 percent. Do not put the plant near radiators. Place a humidifier near the plant or frequently mist it. I keep my misting spray bottle next to the plant and give it a mist throughout the day.

PESTS

Common pests are mealybugs, scale insects, mites, whiteflies, and aphids. Check under the leaves and stems regularly. If pests have occurred, spray with an organic neem oil solution, wash all the leaves with water, and spray again.

DRACAENA TRIFASCIATA (SNAKE PLANT)

The snake plant, also referred to as mother-in-law's tongue, is native to tropical West Africa from Nigeria east to the Congo and will be found in dry, rocky habitats. Like most household succulents, the snake plant helps to filter the air when kept indoors. One particular quality I love is that they are among the few plants that can convert carbon dioxide into oxygen at night. Snake plants are good for plant lovers who have busy lifestyles or like to go away on vacation often. They don't require much attention and their watering schedule is limited, so they are forgiving if watered later than usual.

Snake plants have become a popular houseplant in offices as well as in the home because they are easy to grow and low maintenance. I would consider them hardy as they can put up with almost anything. The snake plant has a very modern harsh look, so it may not be favoured by everyone. It is not the sort of plant that is inviting to touch because of its tough pointed leaves. However, it definitely does not lack character and will look great in any indoor garden.

Snake plants come in many varieties—short or tall, round or flat leaves with variegated patterns and markings—so there is one for everyone and you can choose which best fits your personality. Adding to the convenience, snake plants have a slow growth rate, so repotting will not have to be done often. The leaves are prone to get dusty so keep them dust free by wiping with a damp cloth. With simple care and attention, you can successfully grow the snake plant indoors.

POSITION
They thrive in bright indirect light. Although they can tolerate low light conditions, this will slow down their growth.

WATERING
Water once every two weeks, allowing the soil to completely dry out in between.

SOIL MIX
Snake plants require a well-drained and nutrient-rich potting mix. Use a cactus and succulent mix with a handful of perlite added.

FEEDING
They do not require much fertilizer. Feed once every 4–6 weeks in the growing season using a dilutable liquid fertilizer. Dilute as recommended on the product label.

HUMIDITY
The snake plant can thrive at any humidity, which makes it a good choice to display in the bathroom too.

PESTS
Mealybugs and spider mites are the most common pests. If pests are visible, use an organic neem oil solution with a cotton pad to wipe them off, lightly spraying the plant with the solution after.

POTHOS

Pothos is one of my favorite trailing plants. In fact, it is one of the first indoor plants I ever bought. Native to Southeast Asia, it has become more and more popular. The most common types are the silver pothos (*Scindapsus pictus*) and the golden pothos (*Epipremnum aureum*). The silver pothos has lush green leaves with silvery speckles on them, while the golden pothos has vibrant glossy leaves with shades of yellow on some of the leaves.

Not only do these plants look great, but they are fantastic to have in the home as they are air purifiers, helping to cleanse the air of benzene, formaldehyde, and other harmful substances. However, they can be toxic to pets and humans, so be mindful where you put them.

POSITION

Pothos is very easy to grow indoors and is perfect for vertical gardening, either in a hanging basket or trained up a moss pole. This makes it a great plant if you don't have a lot of indoor space. I like to grow mine in a hanging basket suspended from the ceiling. Using mirrors behind hanging baskets can be an effective touch, increasing light in an otherwise dark corner or just making the plant look fuller. I love how the leaves cascade down so beautifully.

This plant likes bright indirect light but can tolerate lower light conditions too. Because it is so forgiving when it comes to light requirements, it can also make a lovely addition to your bathroom or office.

WATERING

I would suggest watering once a week during the summer months and once every two weeks in the winter. Do be careful not to overwater: curling leaves are a clear indication the plant has been overwatered. Allow the soil to dry in between watering.

SOIL MIX

These plants thrive in well-draining soil. The best I can suggest is 50 percent regular potting compost mixed with 50 percent perlite. Ensure your pot has adequate drainage holes.

FEEDING

Feed your plant every 4 weeks during the growing season. This will encourage healthy new growth and promote lush leaves.

When given the right care conditions, it is a fast grower. To prevent the vines from getting too leggy, I suggest cutting them back at the node (where the leaves emerge from the stem). This will promote bushier growth and will create a better-shaped plant. New growth will start from where you cut the stem.

HUMIDITY

Frequent misting increases the humidity around the plant and keeps the foliage looking its best.

If you decide to have your plant growing up a trellis or moss pole, misting will encourage the aerial roots to attach on to the trellis or moss pole more easily.

PESTS

Mealybugs, spider mites, and scale insects are attracted to pothos. A homemade solution I always use that works at eradicating common plant pests is a basic neem oil insecticide spray. Mix 1 tsp. (6ml) of castile soap and warm water into a 3 oz. (1 L) spray bottle and shake well, then add 4 tsps. (24ml) of neem oil. Spray under the leaves and all stems of the plant. Repeat once a week until the infestation has gone.

QUICK CARE TIPS

- Pothos thrives in bright indirect light but is also tolerant of low light.
- Allow the soil to dry in between watering.
- Mist frequently to raise humidity around the plant and encourage aerial root growth.
- Feed once every 4 weeks in the growing season.
- Toxic to humans and pets.

How to Propagate Pothos

Before you know it, you will be able to propagate your plant, either to create a whole new plant or to make your existing one look fuller. You can enhance the "mother" plant by cutting a stem at a node and simply pushing the cutting back into the pot.

Propagating and rooting are easy because pothos has aerial roots, which grow above the ground and are usually visible as woody growths protruding from the stem. On pothos they look like tiny bumps on the stem. On woody vines, such as English ivy, they function as anchors, fixing themselves onto supporting structures, such as trellises and walls. When these aerial roots make contact with soil or water, they sprout and grow. Some types of aerial roots (such as the ones founds on orchids) absorb water directly from the air.

There are two simple ways to propagate for success every time. For soil propagation you will need a light, well-draining mix. For this you should combine 50 percent regular potting soil with 50 percent perlite.

WATER PROPAGATION

Cut a stem around 6" (15cm) in length, making sure you have four or more leaves on the stem.

Remove the leaf closest to the cut end.

Place the cutting in a glass of water, preferably rainwater, and keep in bright indirect light. Change the water once a week.

In approximately 3 to 4 weeks, roots will form. Once roots are established you can transfer your cutting to a potting soil.

Choose the longest stem.

Cut above and below a node (the point where the leaves emerge from the stem) to create your cuttings.

Each cutting will have a leaf and a node.

Place the leaf stem cuttings in the soil.

Slightly water the soil and the cuttings.

Keep in bright indirect light. After 4 weeks new growth will start to sprout from the cuttings, a sign that roots have formed.

I love how easy pothos plants are to propagate. You can propagate either to create a fuller plant by putting the cuttings back in with the mother plant or to make new plants.

WHAT YOU NEED TO REMEMBER ABOUT AIR-PURIFYING PLANTS

- Check before you buy if the plant you have your eye on is also an air-purifying plant. Not only would you have brought home a stunning new green friend, but it could also have hidden well-being benefits.

- Through photosynthesis, plants convert the carbon dioxide we exhale into fresh oxygen. However, the amount of leaf surface area influences the rate of air purification: the bigger and leafier the plant you choose, the better.

- The plants in this category will help purify and detoxify the air in your living space and office.

- Cut and remove any old dying leaves to encourage new leaf growth.

- Keep leaves dust free by wiping them with a damp cloth once a week.

CHAPTER 3

HUMIDITY-LOVING PLANTS

These plants require higher-than-average indoor humidity levels. Our homes and offices are often dry, but don't be put off by a plant that requires higher humidity to thrive. Remember, a brightly lit bathroom would be the perfect environment, while smaller varieties do well in terrariums. In this chapter I cover their care needs and ways to increase the humidity around your plants so you can grow them successfully indoors.

CLOCKWISE FROM TOP LEFT *Chamaedorea elegans* (parlor palm); *Asparagus setaceus* (asparagus fern); *Begonia maculata* (polka dot begonia); *Syngonium podophyllum* (pink syngonium).

ASPARAGUS SETACEUS (ASPARAGUS FERN)

Asparagus setaceus, commonly known as the asparagus fern, is a gorgeous plant native to southern Africa. Despite its common name, the plant is not a true fern though the leaves resemble fern-like fronds. Asparagus ferns have airy and delicate foliage that bends over gracefully like a fern. I particularly love the feathery and fuzzy leaves, giving the plant a mesmerizing, whimsical appearance. Asparagus ferns come in different sizes; smaller ones work best displayed on a shelf or table. They make a great choice to have on an office desk too.

Asparagus ferns grown indoors take a little more effort. Keeping the humidity level high is a must. The winter months when radiators are on can be a tricky time for this plant. Keep it away from heaters and drafts to avoid drying out the delicate leaves. When given the right care, its twining stems can reach a height of 8 feet (2.5m); an asparagus fern of this size would work best as a floor plant.

Note that asparagus ferns are toxic to animals so be mindful where the plant is displayed. Handling it without gloves can cause skin irritation in humans.

POSITION

Asparagus ferns thrive in dappled shade. Keep out of direct bright sunlight as this will scorch the leaves. They also do well in artificial light.

WATERING

Water regularly so that the soil can stay moist. Be careful not to overwater as this will cause root rot. Yellow leaves are an indication of overwatering. Water less in the winter months.

SOIL MIX

Asparagus ferns like loamy soil, so I recommend using a loam-based potting compost. Loam contains roughly equal proportions of sand, silt, and clay plus organic matter or humus. It is the ideal soil that outdoor gardeners hope to have or achieve. Most potting composts in garden centers are not loam-based; to find one, do some research before shopping.

FEEDING

Feed once a month in the spring and summer months using a dilutable liquid fertilizer. Dilute to half the strength recommended on the product label.

HUMIDITY

They love humidity. Mist frequently; I would suggest daily misting. Alternatively, place near a humidifier or on a pebble tray to raise the humidity.

PESTS

Common pests attracted are aphids, spider mites, black bean aphids, and root mealybugs. There are two options when treating a pest infestation. Hose the whole plant with water, paying particular attention to the undersides of the plant canopy. Or the more drastic measure, depending on how bad the pest outbreak is: simply cut back all of the fronds (stems) to soil level and allow the plant to grow back again.

QUICK CARE TIPS

- *Begonia maculata* can easily be propagated. Simply cut the stem just below the node (where the leaves emerge from the stem), ensuring you have at least one or two leaves attached to the cutting, and put it in water. Make sure the node is submerged in water. Place in indirect sunlight and in 2 weeks roots will emerge. After roots have grown, you can plant the cutting in soil. See pages 18–21 for more detail on how to propagate this plant.

- Increase humidity by frequent misting and/or placing on a pebble tray or near a humidifier.

- Brown leaf edges and tips are an indication that the plant is dehydrated and needs more water.

- Healthy leaves dropping off is a clear sign of overwatering.

BEGONIA MACULATA
(POLKA DOT BEGONIA)

Clay balls

The photogenic *Begonia maculata* is commonly known as the polka dot begonia. These evergreen, humidity-loving perennials are native to the tropical rain forests of Brazil. They have thick cane-like stems that support lush silver-spotted, angel wing–shaped leaves with crimson undersides. Polka dot begonias also have lovely flowers, and if cared for properly, you will be rewarded with their delicate bell-like blooms, which are often red, white, or pink.

Polka dot begonias are one of the most popular houseplants due to their unique aesthetic. I particularly love this plant for its show-stopping foliage, olive green leaves, and contrasting spots that really stand out on any shelf. It is relatively easy to care for when growing indoors. As it is native to the tropics, it requires much higher humidity than some of the other houseplants you may have in your home or office. Nevertheless, don't let that put you off—I have successfully grown it in my home and witnessed it bloom year after year. The polka dot begonia is a relatively fast grower and in my opinion is a fantastic houseplant. It even works well in a terrarium: an indoor miniature garden confined within a glass container, usually without drainage holes. Planting tiny specimens in terrariums is an alternative way to grow plants, creating a miniature ecosystem. The restricted root space will keep them small enough to be comfortable in this special environment.

POSITION
Polka dot begonias thrive in bright indirect light, which will promote strong growth and blooms. Never expose to direct sunlight because that will burn and scorch the leaves.

WATERING
Water regularly because they do not like to stay too dry for long periods of time. The soil should be moist but not soaking wet; allow the top of the soil to dry out before watering. Always ensure the excess water drains out of the pot drainage holes so that the roots do not sit in water.

SOIL MIX
They grow well in loamy soil. Choose a loam-based soil mix with added perlite. As with all indoor plants, make sure the pot it is in has good drainage holes. They are susceptible to root rot, and I like to put clay balls (pictured top right) at the bottom of the pot so that air can circulate around the roots.

FEEDING
Feed every three weeks during the spring and summer months using a liquid fertilizer. Dilute as recommended on the product label. Stop feeding during autumn and winter.

HUMIDITY
Yes, you guessed it, this plant loves humidity. I cannot stress this enough: it requires high-humidity levels as it is not forgiving if they are too low. To raise the humidity, I mist my plant daily, place on a pebble tray, and always ensure the pebble tray is topped up with water. Alternatively, you can put it near a humidifier.

PESTS
Common pests are mealybugs, aphids, spider mites, scale insects, and thrips. To get rid of any pests, use a cotton swab dipped in rubbing alcohol, which kills them instantly. The alcohol will not damage begonias.

CALADIUM (ELEPHANT EAR)

With its stunning leaf patterns and vibrant colors, the caladium is highly photogenic and lends color to any room. It belongs to the Araceae (or arum) family. Because of the shape of its leaves, it is commonly known as "elephant ear" or "angel wings."

Native to South America, caladiums come in many different hues and display gorgeous texture and bursts of color on their foliage. Although they do flower, these unusual tropical plants are usually grown for their incredible display of multicolored leaves.

Caladiums make great indoor plants and are sure to brighten any shelf or plant corner in the home. They are definitely a conversation piece.

When growing indoors, the key to success lies in mimicking the tropical conditions from which they originate.

POSITION

Think about this before you bring your plant home. Caladiums grow best in warm, humid environments, so definitely keep them away from any drafty windows. A bathroom would be perfect for this plant. It requires bright, indirect light (full sun will scorch and wilt its delicate leaves). I keep mine positioned on a shelf in bright indirect light away from any potential drafts, clustered among other humidity-loving plants.

To encourage your caladiums to grow evenly (and not become too leggy), turn them 90 degrees once a week. They will naturally bend and flop toward the light, so turning them prevents them from bending too far over in one position. Please note: do not mistake floppy stems for over- or underwatering. They are naturally floppy!

WATERING

Caladiums are thirsty and prefer a lot of moisture in the soil. Watering with rainwater when the top inch of soil is dry will keep your plant happy. A useful tip for keeping the soil moist at all times but not waterlogged is to put clay balls at the base of the pot. The balls encourage aeration for the roots and allow any excess water to drain away. Once you have a well-drained soil medium, your tubers (similar to bulbs) will be perfectly

happy and will continue to reward you with vigorous growth.

SOIL MIX

Caladiums thrive in rich, moist, well-drained soil. Use a mix that contains coco coir, orchid bark, and perlite. When growing in the home, these plants need pots with good drainage holes.

FEEDING

Feed with a liquid fertilizer once every two weeks during the growing months to encourage lush growth and nourish the tubers for the next growing season.

HUMIDITY

Make sure you provide your caladium with adequate humidity. I would suggest using a pebble tray plus frequent misting (or keep it in the bathroom). Because I like to display my caladiums in the living area, I place them on a saucer filled with clay balls and water. The evaporation will naturally moisten the ambient air and provide the humidity necessary for these gorgeous plants.

It's a good idea to cluster plants that require high humidity together to help the air around them maintain moisture. Don't place your humidity-loving plants among other plants that cannot tolerate getting their foliage wet.

Caladiums will bring a striking pop of color to any indoor space. I love the variety of colors and leaf patterns these glorious plants have to offer. Having them bounce to life only in the spring and summer months makes them even more special.

PESTS

Caladiums are not typically troubled by pests. Any pest outbreak that might occur would be aphids. To get rid of them, simply shower the plant with a gentle stream of water, paying attention to the undersides of the leaves. Water is the only way to get rid of pests as caladium leaves are very thin and sensitive.

DORMANCY

Caladiums go dormant in the winter. This is the natural cycle of the plant (and common to bulbs and tubers). Naturally the older leaves will always die back first, so don't panic when you notice your largest, most stunning, prized leaf start to turn brown and shrivel. Wait for it to become completely brown and snip it off at the base of the stem. This will allow for new leaf growth.

Having shown off its vibrant foliage all spring and summer, getting all of the energy it needs from light, the plant needs to rest and go dormant. When all the leaves have fallen away and new growth has stopped, dormancy has started.

For the next few months all you will have is a pot of soil, so move it to a dark, cool place. The following spring, replant the tubers in fresh potting soil and keep moist. A temperature of around 77°F (25°C) or more is needed for the plant to come out of dormancy.

Once you have replanted the tubers, you can expect them to take 6 to 8 weeks for the first sign of new growth to emerge. Now you can enjoy your flamboyant caladiums once again.

MARANTA LEUCONEURA (PRAYER PLANT)

The unusual *Maranta leuconeura* is my favorite out of all of the species of prayer plants. Native the tropical rain forests in Brazil, the maranta is more commonly referred to as the prayer plant because it closes up its leaves at night like hands in prayer, and then opens up again at dawn. Marantas are often mistaken for calatheas, to which they are closely related.

The daily characteristic movement that marantas and calatheas (see page 117) share is called nyctinasty and is always a joy to witness. Prayer plants have become popular with indoor plant enthusiasts—I couldn't resist buying one to add to my collection. Marantas have unique foliage with leathery leaves that boast lush pink veins; the underside of the leaves is often dark red.

The maranta is a low-growing tropical plant. In the wild it spreads across the rain forest floor, so it would look stunning on a shelf or displayed in a hanging basket. As this plant moves a lot during different times of the day, ensure there is room for it to stretch and move easily.

Marantas love humidity so the main thing to get right is the humidity level. They do require a bit more attention than the average houseplant. If you want a plant with character and are able to meet its needs, then I would definitely suggest giving it a go. It will surely brighten up any indoor area and in my opinion looks like a natural art piece.

Common prayer plants and calathea varieties. These plants are different genus in the same family *(Marantaceae)*.

QUICK CARE TIPS

- Ensure the plant is placed in a space where it has room to move and stretch.
- Keep in bright indirect light—never in direct sun exposure.
- Raise humidity with frequent misting, a humidifier, or place on a pebble tray.
- Use only distilled water or rainwater.
- Keep the soil consistently moist but not soaking wet at all times during the growing season.

Look out for:

- Yellow or brown leaves, an indication that the plant has been overwatered.
- Leaves curling, an indication that the plant is not getting enough water. Also check the humidity level.

POSITION

Prayer plants thrive in bright indirect light. Never expose to direct sunlight as this will scorch their leaves. Although they can tolerate a bit of shade, constant low light conditions will fade their beautiful leaf patterns.

WATERING

When watering, use only distilled water or rainwater as they are sensitive to tap water. Keep the soil moist, but not soaking wet, at all times from spring until autumn. Water less in the winter, about every 1–2 weeks, allowing the soil to dry about halfway down in between watering.

SOIL MIX

Prayer plants have fine roots and a shallow root system so use a well-draining potting mix. A potting soil that contains coco coir, coarse sand, and loam (see page 66) will ensure adequate drainage.

FEEDING

Feed using a liquid fertilizer every two weeks from spring until autumn. Dilute as recommended on the product label.

HUMIDITY

Prayer plants thrive in humid environments above 60 percent. To increase the humidity you can mist frequently, place the plant on a pebble tray, or use a humidifier. Displaying in the humid environment of a brightly lit bathroom is always another option.

PESTS

Common pests are spider mites, mealybugs, and thrips. To remove pests, simply clean the leaves with a damp cloth and a gentle stream of water.

QUICK CARE TIPS

- Larger varieties are best as floor plants.
- Frequently mist to raise the humidity.
- Avoid direct sunlight as this will scorch the leaves.
- Move into a pot one size larger than the one it is in only when the plant has become rootbound.

Look out for:

- Leaves turning yellow, a sign of overwatering.
- Brown leaf tips and edges or drooping plant, a sign of underwatering. Also check the humidity.
- Brown spots on leaves, usually the result of placing in direct sunlight.

CHAMAEDOREA ELEGANS (PARLOR PALM)

The gorgeous tropical *Chamaedorea elegans* is commonly known as the parlor palm. It is a species of small palm tree native to the rain forests of southern Mexico and Guatemala. The parlor palm is a common houseplant and can be easily found in most shops. Luckily for us plant lovers, we are able to have a piece of the rain forest in our indoor spaces, creating a botanical, tropical feel.

They are not only very easy to look after but also have air-purifying qualities, making them a great choice to have at home or in office spaces. Parlor palms come in many different sizes, so they can be displayed on a shelf, table, desk, or as a floor plant in a large pot. Either way there is a perfect-sized variety for everyone.

They are humidity-loving plants so thrive in a moist environment. The great thing about having a parlor palm is that they are low maintenance as long as their basic care needs are met; you can have a healthy specimen for years that will eventually reward you with regular clusters of flowers. In the wild they can grow up to 8 feet (2.5m) tall. Indoors they can reach a respectable height of 24"–36" (60–90cm) after a few years.

Another quality I love about the parlor palm is that it is a slow grower that does best when snug in its pot, so repotting will not have to be done often: approximately once every two years. You only need to move into a pot that is one size larger once the roots have become rootbound—when you can see that the roots have outgrown the nursery pot and entangled themselves around the drainage holes. The plant may become stuck in its pot as the roots have taken over the interior space of the container; in that case, carefully cut around the plastic nursery pot to free the roots.

POSITION

They thrive in bright indirect light. Although tolerant of lower light conditions, bright indirect light is best as this will also encourage flowering. Never place in direct sunlight as this will scorch the leaves.

WATERING

During the summer months water once or twice a week and once every two weeks in the winter. To avoid root rot, ensure any excess water has drained out of the pot drainage holes.

SOIL MIX

When repotting, use a well-draining cactus or palm potting soil.

FEEDING

To keep the parlor palm thriving with healthy growth, feed once every four weeks in the summer months using a liquid fertilizer. Dilute as recommended on the product label. Do not feed during the winter months.

HUMIDITY

The parlor palm thrives in humid environments. Although tolerant of dry air conditions, they may eventually cause brown leaf edges. To achieve healthy lush leaves, mist frequently or place near a humidifier. Alternatively, if there is enough light in the bathroom, you could consider displaying there.

PESTS

Common pests to look out for are mealybugs, spider mites, scale insects, thrips, and whiteflies. If they do occur, use an organic neem oil solution and spray the whole plant. I find it easier to put the plant in the bath and shower down all of the leaves to remove any bugs, then spray with the neem oil solution afterward.

SYNGONIUM (ARROWHEAD PLANT)

Syngonium plants come in many different varieties. Native to the tropical rain forests of the West Indies, southern Mexico, and Central and South America, they are low maintenance with the added benefit of having air-purifying qualities. Syngoniums are commonly known as arrowhead plants as their leaves appear spade-like. My favorite varieties are the pink *Syngonium podophyllum* commonly known as 'Syngonium Blush.' As a group, they are dream plants because of the stunning varieties that are available, making it so tempting to have more than one. Their leaves come in a range of colors and patterns so there is a syngonium for all personalities.

Syngoniums are vining plants and come in many different sizes so you can most certainly find the perfect location to display yours. They are also relatively easy to care for when grown indoors, making this a good choice for any new plant parent. They can be displayed on shelves or hanging baskets as well as strained to attach themselves to a moss pole. I particularly love how versatile they are.

Although sygoniums start as compact, well-formed indoor plants, they like to spread out and extend in all directions. Do bear this in mind and give them space. They are prolific growers, so trim them back to maintain the desired shape. I also like to turn mine around 180 degrees every so often as they tend to bend toward the light.

POSITION

Syngoniums are tolerant of low light but medium to bright indirect light is best to encourage growth and maintain their vibrant coloring. Particularly with pink varieties such as 'Pink Splash' or 'Pink Blush,' if placed in too much bright light the leaves will lose the pink pigment and turn green. Avoid direct sunlight.

WATERING

Allow the soil to dry out partially in between watering. Make sure excess water drains out of the pot drainage holes. Yellow leaves are a sign of overwatering, while brown leaves indicate underwatering.

SOIL MIX

These plants thrive in a chunky, well-draining soil mix. Mix regular potting soil with orchid bark and perlite.

FEEDING

Feed once a month in the growing season with a dilutable liquid fertilizer. Dilute as recommended on the product label. No need to feed the plant in the winter months.

HUMIDITY

Syngoniums thrive in humid environments. Frequently mist the plant or place near a humidifier. I mist my plants twice daily and they love it.

PESTS

Generally, they are pest free. However, if you were to come across any, common pests are mealybugs, aphids, spider mites, and thrips. Simply wash all leaves and stems under a gentle stream of water, paying particular attention to the underside of the leaves. Once rinsed, spray with an organic neem oil solution.

QUICK CARE TIPS

- Syngoniums can be displayed in a variety of ways; decide which way works best for your space. Remember they like to spread out in all directions so give them room to do so.

- Keep in medium or bright indirect light. With pink varieties, bright direct light will cause the leaves to lose their pink pigment.

- Frequently mist to raise the humidity.

- Turn 180 degrees every so often to prevent the stems bending over to the light.

FITTONIA (NERVE PLANT)

Fittonias are commonly known as nerve plants. Native to the tropical rain forests of South America, mainly Peru, they love humidity. They are compact plants with striking patterned foliage and come in many dazzling colors, such as pink, red, blood orange, and bright green. Their small size makes them great plants to display in terrariums or potted with other nerve plants to create a mini garden in a pot. I particularly love how miniature they are and they come in lots of colors and varieties. They are also inexpensive so you can have more than one. Their size also makes it easy to find a home for them no matter how limited your space. You can put them in hanging baskets, on small shelves, in terrariums, or on window sills (not south facing). When given the right care and conditions, they can grow to 6" (15cm) tall and can trail to 4" (10cm) long.

Growing nerve plants indoors couldn't be easier. The main elements to get right are the lighting and humidity. They thrive in humid environments and without high humidity they will shrivel and die. Consider displaying them in the bathroom as an option. In the right conditions they grow quickly. If you find that yours is growing too leggy, you can pinch back the stems to encourage new growth and create a bushier plant.

POSITION

Nerve plants thrive in bright indirect light. Do not place in direct sunlight, as this will turn the leaves brown and crispy. Not enough light will cause the vibrant colors on the leaves to fade.

WATERING

During the growing season, water every 3–4 days, allowing the soil to dry out in between watering. During the winter months, water once every 10 days. Do not allow the plant to sit in water.

SOIL MIX

Nerve plants grow best in a well-draining soil. Use a loamy soil that includes coarse sand or perlite to ensure it does not become waterlogged.

FEEDING

Feed once a month in the growing season using a liquid fertilizer. Dilute as recommended on the product label.

HUMIDITY

Nerve plants thrive in humid environments of around 60–70 percent. Raise the humidity around the plant with daily misting, adding a humidifier or placing on a pebble tray. If you have more than one humidity-loving plant indoors, cluster the nerve plant among them.

PESTS

Common pests are mealybugs, aphids, spider mites, scale insects, thrips, and aphids. These are easily eradicated by thoroughly washing all the leaves and stems with water and spraying with an organic neem oil solution.

QUICK CARE TIPS

- Display in hanging baskets or on the side of a bookshelf so that it can cascade.
- Place in bright indirect light, never direct sunlight.
- Mist daily to give the plant the humidity it requires.
- Trim to encourage bushier growth. Trim sparingly as it flowers from the tips of the vine.

AESCHYNANTHUS (LIPSTICK PLANT)

This tropical beauty is commonly known as the lipstick plant, as its unusual pointed flowers resemble dangling lipstick. Native to Malaysia, it thrives in humid environments. Lipstick plants can be found in many different species such as *Aeschynanthus japhrolepsis*, *A. radicans*, and *A. longicaulis*, to name a few. With a cascading, vine-like habit, they make a great choice to have displayed in a hanging basket. Because they need humidity, consider hanging yours in a brightly lit bathroom!

A striking evergreen, given the right care your lipstick plant will reward you with clusters of flowers. Typically, they bloom most abundantly in the summer and autumn. Their flowers are often red but rarer varieties can be found with dark red, yellow, orange, and even coral blooms.

In my experience some species are fast growers, such as *A. japhrolepsis*. Stems can grow to 24" (60cm) or even longer, so they will most definitely add a tropical vibe to any indoor space. The vines can grow very long, so trim to promote bushier growth and keep the desired length. Snip the ends sparingly, as flowering occurs at the tips of the vines.

Although the lipstick plant is easy to grow, do pay attention to its light requirements and humidity levels.

POSITION

Keep in bright indirect light. Never expose it to bright direct light as that will scorch the leaves. Low light conditions will not promote healthy leaf growth and no flowering will occur.

WATERING

Allow the top quarter of soil to dry before watering—this actually promotes blooming. During the growing season you may have to water around once a week. During autumn and winter, the plant will slow down its growth; water every 2–3 weeks.

SOIL MIX

The lipstick plant requires well-draining soil. Use a mix which contains 1 part regular potting mix, 1 part coco coir, and 1 part perlite.

FEEDING

During spring and summer, feed every two weeks using a dilutable liquid fertilizer. Dilute as recommended on the product label. There is no need to feed the plant in autumn and winter.

HUMIDITY

Lipstick plants like warm, humid environments. Mist frequently and keep away from drafts and radiators. It's easier to mist the plant when displayed in a hanging basket. Alternatively, you can keep it in the bathroom, providing there is enough light.

PESTS

Keep an eye out for spider mites, mealybugs, aphids, whiteflies, scale insects, and thrips. To get rid of pests, simply shower down all of the stems and leaves with a gentle stream of water. I would suggest hanging the plant over the bath for this, as the vines can be quite long. Once rinsed, spray (including under leaves) with an organic neem oil solution.

CHLOROPHYTUM COMOSUM (SPIDER PLANT)

Native to South Africa, *Chlorophytum comosum* is commonly known as the spider plant because its naturally occurring babies (or spiderettes) dangle down from the mother plant like a spider's web. This striking plant is also very easy to care for, so it makes a great choice for any new plant parent.

Spider plants can be found in many different sizes; they do tend to grow long, so are best suited as hanging plants. The leaves, which can be up to 36" (90cm) long, tend to grow upward and then bend down in an arc, while the base of the plant can reach around 12" (30cm). If you would like your spider plant to look bushier, you can fill it out by trimming the spiderettes and planting them back in with the mother plant.

Spider plants prefer to be semi-rootbound, so repotting will not need to be done often. Only repot when the plant has got too large for its pot or when the roots are highly visible.

Propagating is very easy. Cut off one of the spiderettes and plant it in well-drained soil that is kept consistently moist. Cover the pot in a plastic bag with holes in it for ventilation and keep in a bright location (but out of direct sunlight). Once the baby plant is well rooted (look for signs of new growth), remove the bag and grow as usual.

Spider plants love humidity, so to grow them successfully ensure the humidity levels are high.

POSITION

They thrive in bright indirect light, where the striping on the leaves will be more prominent. Avoid direct sunlight as this will scorch the leaves.

WATERING

Water once a week in the spring and summer months. During the winter allow the soil to dry slightly in between watering. Spider plants are sensitive to tap water so use rainwater or distilled water.

SOIL MIX

Spider plants prefer a loamy, well-draining soil. If you are mixing your own, you can combine regular loam-based compost with perlite.

FEEDING

Spider plants are prone to get leaf burn when overfed. I suggest feeding only once a month in the spring and summer. When feeding certain plants, to avoid leaf burn and to be on the safe side, I always dilute my liquid fertilizer to half the strength that is recommended on the product label. With the spider plant it's better to underfeed.

HUMIDITY

The ideal humidity level is 60 percent or above. In warmer environments they can thrive at humidity levels of 40 percent. Use a humidifier or mist frequently. If there is enough light in the bathroom, consider hanging yours there.

PESTS

They are not particularly prone to pests, which is great to know. However, if they do get an infestation the common pests are scale, aphids, spider mites, and whiteflies. Hose down the leaves with water and then spray the whole plant with an organic neem oil solution.

- Spider plants tend to grow long, so are best displayed in a hanging basket.

- Do not use tap water; distilled water or rainwater is essential.

- For convenience, display in a brightly lit bathroom to give your plant the humidity it requires. Alternatively, use a humidifier or mist frequently.

- Create a bushier plant by cutting off the babies from the mother plant, then replanting them in with her.

- Only repot if the plant has outgrown its pot or the roots are highly visible.

QUICK CARE TIPS

- Position in bright indirect light.
- It likes a warm environment, so keep away from drafts.
- Keep soil evenly moist, and don't allow the soil to dry out completely.

Look out for:

- Leaf curling or leaf drop, caused by a sudden drop in temperature or low humidity levels.
- Pests, check under leaves weekly.

CISSUS DISCOLOR (REX BEGONIA VINE)

Cissus discolor, pronounced KISS-us, DIS-kol-or, is one of my favorites when it comes to indoor gardening. This stunning foliage plant belongs to the *Vitaceae* (grape) family. Native to China, India, and Indonesia, it is commonly known as the rex begonia vine although it is not actually a begonia and should not be confused with the similar-sounding rex (or king) begonia (*Begonia rex*) on pages 130–31. (Confusingly similar common names are a good illustration of how useful and important botanical names are in uniquely identifying every plant.) Its rich, velvety textured leaves boast vivid purple and lush shades of green with a deep burgundy red tone under the leaf; when looked at in the light you can catch a slight shimmer of silver on the leaf surface, making this plant a joy to have in the home.

Cissus discolor is a great indoor plant for the new plant parent, as it is easy to maintain and requires minimal attention. It thrives in humid environments; the main factor to get right when growing indoors is the humidity level.

Thanks to its large, striking foliage and climbing abilities, *Cissus discolor* has become a popular houseplant. It grows really well in pots or a hanging basket; it can also climb up trellises. Do think about the space you have available, whether displayed hanging or climbing, as it can grow up to 6–8 feet (1.8–2.5m). Its velvety leaves are typically 3"–6" (7–15cm) long.

Overall, whether you decide you want it hanging beautifully or vining up a trellis, by ensuring you meet all the basic care needs of this plant you will surely be rewarded and delighted with its gorgeous foliage.

POSITION

Cissus discolor grows best in bright indirect light or filtered light and needs warm temperatures to thrive.

One thing to look out for is leaf curling or leaves dropping off. This only happens with a sudden drop in temperature, so you need to keep this plant away from any drafts.

WATERING

It does not like saturated soil and definitely cannot tolerate its fine roots sitting in water. The basic rule of thumb is to water generously once a week in the summer months and allow the top inch of soil to dry out during the winter months. I water mine by filling up a watering can and pouring over the soil completely until water starts to drip out of the drainage holes, waiting for all of that excess water to drain away before placing it back in its decorative pot; that way you can ensure the roots are not sitting in water.

SOIL MIX

The best soil for this plant is nutrient rich but also well draining. Use a mix with 50 percent regular potting soil, 40 percent perlite, and 10 percent sphagnum moss. (See page 17 for a note on the difference between sphagnum moss and sphagnum peat moss.)

FEEDING

Feed every 3–4 weeks during the spring, summer, and autumn.

HUMIDITY

Mist the plant daily to raise the humidity level. Curling brown leaf edges are a sign that the humidity level is too low.

PESTS

Common pests include whiteflies, mealybugs, and red spider mites. To get rid of pests use an organic neem oil solution and spray the whole plant, paying particular attention to the underside of the leaves.

How to Propagate
Cissus discolor

What I love about *Cissus discolor* is that it wants to grow and vine, so in no time you will have new vines sprouting, which mean more lush leaves. As one of the easiest plants in this book to propagate, you can make these vines into new plants, which is always so rewarding.

Propagate this plant from either stem cuttings in water or leaf cuttings in sphagnum moss.

1   WATER PROPAGATION

Cut a vine that has four leaves on it. Cut off the lowest leaf to expose the node (the point where leaves emerge from the stem).

Place the stem cutting in a glass of rainwater, making sure that the node is submerged, and keep in a warm place that gets a lot of bright indirect light. Change the water once a week.

In approximately 3–5 weeks the roots should be long enough to transfer into your soil mixture.

Prepare a large shallow container with damp sphagnum moss.

Take a long vine cutting with approximately 8–10 leaves.

Cut the vine in between each leaf to create a leaf stem cutting.

Dip your leaf stem cutting in rooting hormone powder (see page 21).

Push down the cutting into the sphagnum moss; repeat this with all of your leaf cuttings, ensuring the stem is snug.

Once they are all in the sphagnum moss, mist slightly to create a humid environment.

Place a lid or cling film over the propagation tray (if using cling film, pierce a few holes for ventilation). This will keep the air inside the container nice and humid so the cuttings can root.

Place your container in a warm area with bright indirect light. You will not need to water your cuttings again throughout this period as sphagnum moss retains water. Within 5 weeks you will have roots growing from your cuttings and maybe a new vine forming.

After roots are established, it's time to move your leaf cuttings into your potting mixture. Lightly moisten the soil and place the pot in bright indirect light.

Here is a fittonia that I have planted in a mini hanging pot. Fittonias do well in terrariums too (see opposite). Remember to mist them frequently but to avoid the soil getting waterlogged. I spray the soil and leaves till moist. Allow the soil to dry before spraying again.

WHAT YOU NEED TO REMEMBER ABOUT HUMIDITY-LOVING PLANTS

- Sudden leaf drop of healthy leaves after you have just brought your new plant home is very common. This is due to the sudden change in environment. Your plant is in shock and needs to adapt to its new home, so give it a few days and it will bounce back into life.

- Increase humidity around your plants by using a pebble tray, humidifier or frequent misting. You can also increase humidity by grouping plants together. Remember the bathroom is a humid environment, so consider displaying them in there too!

- Look out for brown, crispy leaf edges. This is a clear indication that the humidity around the plant needs to be raised.

- Some plants, such as the caladium, thrive in soil that is moist at all times but not waterlogged. A great tip to avoid waterlogging is to put clay balls at the base of the pot.

- To encourage balanced, even growth and prevent bent-over stems, turn your plants 90 degrees once a week.

- Don't be afraid to snip off any unhealthy and unattractive leaves. Your plant will benefit from having dead leaves removed as this will encourage new healthy growth.

CHAPTER 4

HEAT-TOLERANT PLANTS

Plants in this chapter can thrive in warm environments and also require minimal water. If you go on vacation often, these plants are ideal. Cacti and succulents come in so many sizes and varieties. If you are on the lookout for miniature plants with lots of character, they will be your best friends. Number one rule: go easy on the watering.

Kalanchoe tomentosa (panda plant); *Crassula ovata* (jade plant); *Echeveria* ('Blue Bird').

ALOE VERA

Aloe vera is one of the most common and easily recognizable indoor plants. It is native to North Africa, southern Europe, and the Canary Islands. I particularly love how easy it is to care for and as an added bonus it has air-purifying qualities. It is also heat tolerant so growing in warm indoor environments with direct sun exposure will not kill it. In fact, *Aloe vera* thrives in direct sunlight.

   Aloe vera can be found in many different varieties. Some have speckled leaf patterns, smooth or spiky leaf edges, but all create perfectly symmetrical leaf formations. It can also come in many different sizes. Miniature varieties are always more convenient displayed on window sills, and because they are so small you can have more than one. Larger ones are best on shelves, tables, or desks. On their own they almost look like living art pieces. These stemless plants that boast thick green fleshy leaves add a modern feel to any indoor setting.

   Aloe vera is a great choice to brighten up offices spaces as well as the home. Meet its very minimal needs and you will soon be rewarded with small "pups," which can easily be removed from the mother plant and put into their own nursery pot.

POSITION

It thrives in full sunlight, bright, or indirect light conditions. Low light will cause the plant to grow leggy and limp and bend toward any light source, which will create an uneven shape. *Aloe vera* grows best in temperatures from 55–80°F (13–27°C). The main thing to get right is the sunlight exposure as it loves the sun.

WATERING

Water every 2–3 weeks during the spring and summer months. Water even more sparingly during autumn and winter. I like to double the amount of time in between watering during the winter months. So if you water once every 3 weeks during the summer, make it every 6 weeks in the winter.

SOIL MIX

It requires a well-draining soil to reduce the risk of root rot: use a regular potting soil mixed with coarse sand and perlite.

FEEDING

Feed once in the spring using a liquid fertilizer diluted as recommended on the product label. I would suggest watering the plant thoroughly the day before feeding. This will flush out any salt residues and reduce the risk of the leaf tips burning.

HUMIDITY

Average indoor environments are fine for *Aloe vera*. No extra humidity is needed.

PESTS

Aloe mites and mealybugs are attracted to this plant. They are easy to get rid of: simply use a mixture of castile soap and water to clean all of the fleshy leaves and then rinse with water. (To make your own insecticidal soap spray, combine 1 Tbsp. (15ml) of castile soap with 3 oz. (1 L) of water; shake well and use immediately.)

CACTI

Cactus plants are known for their sun-loving nature but they can thrive indoors. Native to the Americas ranging from Patagonia in the south to western Canada in the north, they have become a trendy indoor plant and are all individually striking and unique in their own way, adding character to any indoor space.

There are two groups grown as houseplants: desert and forest cacti. Desert cacti are the more traditional ones, which are easily recognized by their spines and hairs. Forest cacti grow in woody subtropical environments; the well-known Christmas cactus is one of these.

Luckily for us houseplant lovers, cacti can be found in many different sizes, making it easier to find the perfect location. I particularly love the miniature varieties; their size means I can have lots of them as they are all so adorable it's hard to choose. They are very low maintenance so make a great choice for the new plant parent or anyone who has a busy lifestyle with limited time to dedicate to plants.

Cacti can be positioned pretty much anywhere indoors—just make sure that there is ample light and the environment is warm. One characteristic I love about them is that many varieties flower. I love to see cacti in bloom, when the tiny vibrant flowers soften the often hard, spiky exterior of the plant.

POSITION

They thrive in bright light. Place in or near a south-facing window to keep them happy.

WATERING

During the spring, summer, and autumn months water every 7–10 days. Ensure excess water has drained out of the pot drainage holes so that the roots do not sit in water. They are drought tolerant so don't worry if you miss a watering, as they are very forgiving. During the winter months reduce watering to every 4–6 weeks.

SOIL MIX

The perfect repotting soil is a mix that contains 3 parts regular potting soil, 3 parts coarse sand or gravel, and 2 parts perlite. Alternatively you can purchase a readily available cactus potting mix. That way you can be sure the soil mix is perfect for your cactus.

FEEDING

Cacti are not heavy feeders. Feed once a year in spring to encourage blooming. Use a liquid fertilizer, diluted to half the strength suggested on the product label.

HUMIDITY

Species of desert cacti, such as the barrel cactus, thrive in average indoor humidity levels and even in dry-air conditions. Species of forest cacti, such as the Christmas cactus, thrive in average-to-high humidity levels.

PESTS

The most common pests are mealybugs, scale insects, spider mites, and fungus gnats. They can easily be removed either by using rubbing alcohol on a cotton pad or by spraying an organic neem oil solution onto the entire plant. I prefer the neem oil method, as most cacti have spikes that make them tricky to clean with a cotton swab.

SUCCULENTS

Succulents are another group that have grown in popularity as houseplants. They particularly love warm environments so growing them indoors is perfect. Succulents are native to dry areas—deserts and semi-deserts—and can also be found in mountainous regions and rain forests. They boast eye-catching plump foliage with gorgeous leaf shapes and striking textures that transform them into living sculptures, adding character to any indoor setting. Succulents can be found in many species and varieties, such as *Sedum bulbiferum* and my favorite *Echeveria pulvinata*, and most often they will be found in miniature-sized pots. Miniature plants are a plant lover's dream, especially for me, as it means I can have lots of the same plant without them taking up too much space.

Believe it or not, the most common problem people have when caring for succulents is watering. A lot of people tend to treat succulents as if they are cacti and water too sparingly, or else they treat them like regular houseplants and end up unintentionally overwatering. Succulents store water in their plump foliage, so when you are growing them you must water each plant according to its soil moisture level. They cannot be watered on a schedule!

Succulents are a great choice for office desks, indoor shelving, and window sills. They can be positioned pretty much anywhere in the home that has adequate lighting. What I love about them is how creative you can be. They have shallow root systems so they can easily be removed from their nursery pots and clustered together into shallow bowls or ornamental containers to create a mini plant world. This is a particularly good project to gets kids involved with—my daughter certainly loves getting her hands dirty with plant decor/care!

POSITION

Typically, succulents need at least between 4 and 6 hours of sunlight per day to grow and mature. Note that lower light levels will slow down growth. A brightly lit window will keep them happy as long as it is not cold or drafty. During the winter, daylight will be shorter, so position them in the brightest location or under a grow light to give them the light they need.

WATERING

Before watering, check the soil first. Allow it to dry completely in between watering; ensure that the pot feels light first. That being said, do not let plants remain in dry soil conditions for days—they are not cacti and will quickly shrivel.

Succulents store a lot of water in the leaves so be careful not to overwater. With all succulents I use the bottom-up method by placing the pot on a saucer of water so that it is 25 percent submerged. Allow the roots to suck up as much water as the plant needs; that way you won't overwater. Let it sit in the water for 5–15 minutes or until the top of the soil feels slightly damp to the touch; refill the saucer with water if needed.

SOIL MIX

Succulents require a well-draining soil. Cactus compost is ideal; alternatively, you can create your own succulent soil medium. Just mix of 3 parts regular potting compost with 2 parts sharp sand and 1 part perlite.

FEEDING

They are not heavy feeders. Once a year in spring, use a fertilizer diluted to half the strength recommended on the product label. Spring is the beginning of their growing season for a lot of succulents so they will most definitely benefit from the added nutrients.

HUMIDITY

Succulents can thrive in average indoor humidity levels.

PESTS

Common pests are spider mites, aphids, and fungus gnats. To eradicate pests on succulents, use an insecticidal soap solution. Combine 1 Tbsp. (15ml) of castile soap with 3 oz. (1 L) of water; shake well and use immediately. Apply it on to the plant with a cotton ball.

ABOVE *Crassula ovata* (jade plant); *Crassula ovata* 'Gollum' (jade fingers plant); *Crassula arborescens* (ripple jade). OPPOSITE *Echeveria* 'Blue prince.'

WHAT YOU NEED TO REMEMBER ABOUT HEAT-TOLERANT PLANTS

- *Aloe vera*, cacti, and succulents all have fleshy stems that contain water. Water these plants sparingly to avoid overwatering.
- Use a well-draining porous soul for the plants in this section.
- They all have a unique sculptural aesthetic, brightening up any indoor space. These plants are a great choice to have on office desks too.
- Cacti and succulents are easy to find as miniature plants, which is great for us plant lovers as it means we can have more than one!

CHAPTER 5

PLANTS TO HELP WITH PESTS

With increasing demand for rare and unusual indoor plants, nurseries and garden centers are making them much more available to plant lovers. On social media I have witnessed carnivorous plants grow in popularity, and people are not daunted by their specific care needs. We plant lovers can have the pleasure of growing these fascinating plants with the added benefit of them minimizing pests in our indoor gardens. Not all carnivorous plants are suitable houseplants, but here are three that will do well indoors.

Nepenthes alata
(tropical pitcher plant).

DIONAEA MUSCIPULA (VENUS FLYTRAP)

The Venus flytrap is probably the most famous and recognizable carnivorous plant. Charles Darwin famously described it as "one of the most wonderful in the world," and those of you who have witnessed the plant snap and catch its prey would likely agree.

Native to North and South Carolina, it is a fun addition to your indoor garden. Not only is it interesting to have, but it will also help get rid of flies and fungus gnats hovering around your other plants. These pests are attracted to the nectar on its opening traps, and once they land on the leaves, they stimulate the trigger hairs, causing the trap to close around the insect.

Venus flytraps are relatively easy to care for indoors. In their natural environment, they grow in acidic bogs: soil that is moist at all times. Unlike other plants, they thrive in poor soil that lacks nutrients. By mimicking this within the home, you can grow these fascinating plants successfully.

We all get such great satisfaction from Venus flytraps, and I know how tempting it is to play with them, mimicking a fly to get the trap to close. However, I would strongly advise against doing this as closing the trap requires a lot of plant energy. Eventually, it can kill your plant by depleting all of the energy reserves it needs to grow.

Overall, the Venus flytrap as an indoor plant is a joy to have and fun for children and the whole family to enjoy.

POSITION

Position in bright indirect artificial light or bright indirect sunlight; it performs well at average indoor temperatures.

WATERING

Keep well watered so that the soil is moist at all times—never allow it to completely dry out. When watering the Venus flytrap and all carnivorous plants, be sure to use only distilled water or rainwater. I cannot stress this enough. Rainwater and distilled water have few nutrients, while tap water and mineral water have traces of minerals that will kill your carnivorous plants.

SOIL MIX

They need nutrient-free soil that provides good drainage. I would suggest buying a specialized carnivorous plant potting compost. The texture almost resembles a dark, gritty, bad-quality sand, but don't be put off—this is the best soil for them and what they thrive in.

FEEDING

As with all carnivorous plants, Venus flytraps get their nutrients from the insects they catch, which is why it's so important that the soil and water have no nutrients. Giving them nutrients would prevent them from growing more traps; starving the plant of nutrients encourages it to grow.

Having the Venus flytrap positioned among your other houseplants will help to get rid of those pesky fungus gnats and flies. However, if there are no flies available for them to catch, you can feed them dried mealworms. A mealworm one-third the size of the trap is the perfect portion. Feeding one trap per week is the right amount of meaty nutrients. You will notice that the plant grows in clusters, so feed only one of the traps in a cluster. One thing to remember: dried mealworms are hard, so be sure to soak them in distilled water or rainwater the night before to soften them.

HUMIDITY

Luckily, the Venus flytrap can thrive and be happy with average indoor humidity levels, so misting is not a necessity.

NEPENTHES (TROPICAL PITCHER PLANT)

Mostly native to Madagascar, Southeast Asia, and Australia, nepenthes is commonly known as the tropical pitcher plant or monkey cups, which comes from monkeys occasionally drinking water from the hanging pitchers (cups).

Out of all carnivorous plants, this is my favorite. I love how unusual it looks and I like to have mine displayed in a hanging basket. As with the Venus flytrap, flies and fungus gnats are attracted to the nectar secretions, but they are also attracted to the coloration of the pitcher. Once flies fall into the pitcher, they are consumed by the digestive juices at the bottom. Having nepenthes among your other houseplants will definitely help get rid of these pests.

When growing in the home the main elements to success are adequate light and high humidity, and the soil should be kept moist at all times. Although native to lowland steamy jungles, nepenthes can be grown successfully indoors and will be sure to add joy and wonder to any indoor garden.

When pitchers start to shrivel and get crispy, it's time to cut them off to save plant energy, which will promote more pitcher growth. Simply get a sharp pair of scissors and snip the pitcher at the top of the stem where it meets the leaf. When you notice leaves turning yellow, this is completely normal; those are the older, more mature leaves dying off.

Given the right care and conditions, nepenthes should be given a chance. Children will definitely enjoy getting involved in its care and feeding, and it is a fun interactive plant to have within the home.

POSITION

Nepenthes thrives in bright light so be sure to position in the brightest location you have (but not direct sun). Grow lights can be helpful.

WATERING

When it comes to watering, as with all carnivorous plants, they require moist soil that should not be left to dry out. However, they are not bog plants so don't want to be waterlogged. Only use rainwater or distilled water as they will perish if watered with tap water or mineral water.

SOIL MIX

They are tolerant of a variety of soil mixes; however, I would suggest using a specialized carnivorous potting mix so you can be certain it has the right level of acidity and is nutrient free.

FEEDING

As with the Venus flytrap, nepenthes can be fed dried mealworms if there are no flies around to catch. This is a really good way of keeping your plant's nutrient levels up, ensuring it is not starved of the nutrients it needs to survive.

Feeding a few dried mealworms into a couple of the pitchers every 2–3 weeks is sufficient and will most certainly keep your pitcher plant happy and healthy. Dried mealworms must be soaked in rainwater or distilled water to soften them before feeding to the plant; otherwise, they won't be able to absorb the nutrients.

HUMIDITY

Keeping the humidity levels up can be done with frequent misting or using a humidifier. If you notice your plant is not growing pitchers, this is a clear sign that either it isn't getting enough light or the humidity level isn't high enough.

QUICK CARE TIPS

- Keep in bright light.
- Keep soil moist at all times.
- Mist frequently to increase humidity.
- Cut off old pitchers to promote more growth.
- Feed dried mealworms (softened first) if there are no pests to catch.

SARRACENIA (TRUMPET PITCHER PLANT)

This insect eater is a bog plant, indigenous to Texas, southeastern Canada, and the eastern seaboard of the United States. Belonging to the *Sarraceniaceae* family, sarracenia is commonly known as the trumpet pitcher plant. It looks stunning displayed on any plant shelf. Its deep red veins, creating a speckled print on the trumpet pitchers, really do make it fascinating and beautiful. It is also easy to care for.

Sarracenia (like nepenthes) lures its prey with the sap it secretes. The slippery rim of the trumpet makes it very easy for an insect to slip inside, where the sticky walls trap the prey until it falls into the digestive fluids at the bottom. This is how the plant gets all the nutrients it needs to thrive. I place my sarracenia among other houseplants to help keep them free from flies and fungus gnats.

Overall, this carnivorous plant is relatively easy to care for.

QUICK CARE TIPS

- Keep in the brightest location in the home.
- Water with rainwater or distilled water only.
- Keep the humidity high around the plant.
- Ensure the plant is sitting in water constantly.
- If there are no flies or fungus gnats around, feed bugs, fish food, or dried mealworms (soaked first).

POSITION

It is naturally found in bogs or marshes that are constantly damp, so these conditions need to be replicated. It is also sun-loving so will need to be positioned in the brightest possible position within your home. It needs normal-to-warm indoor temperatures.

WATERING

Keeping the soil wet (using rainwater or distilled water only) is a must. Try to ensure the plant is sitting in water constantly; you can even have the base of the pot in water, recreating its native bog conditions.

SOIL MIX

As with other plants in this chapter, sarracenia thrives in acidic soil. I suggest purchasing readily available compost for carnivorous plants. That way you can be sure the soil is perfect for your plant pets.

FEEDING

If there are no flies around for the plant to catch, it will be starved of the nutrients it needs to survive. Fortunately, however, sarracenia can easily be fed manually. Simply drop bugs, fish food, or dried mealworms into a few of the trumpets every two to three weeks. If using dried mealworms, soak in rainwater to soften them so that the plant can absorb the nutrients.

HUMIDITY

As it thrives in humid environments, a brightly lit bathroom, where it will benefit from the humidity and steam, would be an ideal location. However, there are other ways to give the plant the conditions it requires. To keep the humidity levels high, you can either mist frequently or place on a pebble tray.

I like to dress the top of the soil with damp sphagnum moss. This helps to lock moisture into the soil and at the same time increases humidity around the plant.

Nepenthes has become increasingly popular as an indoor plant. I love how it brings a whimsical and playful element to my indoor garden. The Venus flytrap (opposite) is another fun plant and instantly recognizable.

WHAT YOU NEED TO REMEMBER ABOUT PLANTS TO HELP WITH PESTS

- Carnivorous plants thrive in moist, bog-like soil, so never let them dry out.
- Use a specialized carnivorous potting mix for your carnivorous plants.
- Only rainwater or distilled water must be used. This is because tap or mineral water has too many trace minerals, such as chloride and fluoride, which build up as salts in the soil and will eventually kill your plant.
- If no flies are around for your carnivorous plants to catch, you can feed them dried mealworms. Remember to soak the mealworms in water first to soften them.
- As tempting as it is, do not play with the traps on the Venus flytrap. This will deplete the plant's energy.
- Snip off any old yellow leaves and crispy pitchers (traps) to encourage new leaf and pitcher growth.

CHAPTER 6

DIVA PLANTS

You guessed it—this chapter is called "Diva Plants" because they are little divas that can be high maintenance. Plants in this section require a lot more attention and all have very specific care needs. They are for the more experienced plant parent who has the time and patience to cater for their very individual requirements. Don't be put off; with my very easy-to-digest care instructions you can feel confident about growing these plants successfully.

CLOCKWISE FROM TOP LEFT *Calathea warscewiczii* (jungle velvet); *Calathea makoyana* (peacock plant); Calathea Medallion (rose-painted calathea); *Calathea ornata* (pinstripe calathea).

ALOCASIA X AMAZONICA (ELEPHANT EAR)

Alocasia x *amazonica* is commonly known as either African mask or elephant ear. Native to Southeast Asia, these plants grow in subtropical areas. In the wild they are found on forest floors and become a lot larger in their natural habitat than they do indoors. I have seen elephant ear grow in popularity as an indoor plant over the years on social media. It is stunning and unusual with bold, attractive, shiny, waxy leaves with deep silver-white veins. Each leaf can grow to 12" (30cm) in length, adding an abstract design quality to any indoor space.

Elephant ear plants are not for the new plant parent. They really are "diva plants" that require all care conditions to be perfect. Make one mistake and they will most definitely let you know! Although not easy, they are worth purchasing if you can provide what they need. Be mindful of where you display them as they are toxic to both humans and pets. Get their particular care needs right and you will be rewarded in abundance.

QUICK CARE TIPS

- Keep the leaves dust free by gently wiping down with a damp cloth.
- Raise the humidity with frequent misting or place on a pebble tray.
- Ensure the soil is moist but not soaking wet.
- Toxic to humans and pets.

Look out for:

- Browning leaves could be a result of insufficient humidity, exposure to direct sunlight, or dry soil.
- It is sensitive to cold. Leaf spots will occur if room temperatures drop below 59°F (15°C).

POSITION

Elephant ear thrives in medium to bright indirect light; it is not suited for low light conditions. Do not expose to direct sunlight as this can scorch the leaves.

WATERING

Keep the soil moist but not wet. In the winter months allow the top 2" (5cm) of soil to dry out between watering to prevent root rot.

SOIL MIX

The most important factor in successful growth is the soil, which needs to be porous. I recommend a potting mix of 1 part regular potting soil, 1 part perlite, and 1 part coco coir. This will be well drained and aerated yet can remain moist. It has worked a treat for me.

FEEDING

It doesn't have any specific feeding needs. You can feed once a month in the spring and summer with a dilutable liquid fertilizer.

Dilute to half the strength recommended on the product label. Feeding during the winter won't be necessary.

HUMIDITY

Alocasia 'Polly' thrives in humid environments. Mist daily or place on a pebble tray to increase the humidity.

TEMPERATURE

Temperatures ranging from 65–77°F (18–25°C) are required; avoid sudden changes and cold drafts. Temperatures above and below this range can cause damage to the plant, first evident when healthy leaves start to droop.

PESTS

Common pests to look out for are mealybugs, scale insects, aphids, and spider mites. To get rid of any pests, spray with an organic neem oil solution, paying extra attention to the underside of the leaves.

CALATHEA (PRAYER PLANT)

Calatheas have become one of the most sought-after indoor plants in recent years, and I have witnessed them grow in huge popularity on social media. Native to the jungles in South America, they come in many varieties, each boasting lush patterned foliage which makes them by far one of the most attractive indoor plants. Calatheas are closely related to marantas (see page 74), and you will notice that they share the same movement characteristic known as nyctinasty, where the leaves open wide during the day and fold inward at night.

Calatheas have gained a reputation for being somewhat fussy about their growing conditions; however, the dazzling, boldly marked leaves are so stunning that plant lovers cannot resist bringing one home. Having one of these beauties will quite literally be like bringing a piece of the jungle indoors. They look striking clustered among other humidity-loving plants as well as on their own as an eye-catching statement plant.

They are very sensitive to chilly temperatures or any sudden change in indoor temperature, and grow best in warm, humid environments. But don't be put off by their fussy reputation. Given the right care and growing conditions, they are fast growers and beautiful plants to have in any indoor setting.

POSITION
Calatheas thrive in bright indirect light. Never position in direct sunlight as this will burn the leaves and also cause them to lose their vibrant colors. Faded leaf color is an indication that the plant is receiving too much light.

WATERING
When watering, use distilled water or rainwater as they are sensitive to the chemicals in tap water. Watering will generally be needed once a week. Check the top 2" (5cm) of soil to see that it is dry before watering. Always allow excess water to drain out of the pot drainage holes, making sure the plant is never sitting in water, to prevent root rot.

SOIL MIX
Calatheas have definitely earned the right to be in the diva chapter as even their soil has to be just right! They need it to be moist but not soaking wet. The best medium is 50 percent regular potting compost mixed with 20 percent charcoal, 20 percent orchid bark, and 10 percent perlite.

FEEDING
Only feed once a month during the spring and summer months using a dilutable liquid fertilizer. Use half the strength recommended on the product label to prevent leaf burn. It's always better to be on the safe side and underfeed rather than overfeed.

HUMIDITY
Calatheas require high humidity. You can increase the humidity around the plant by placing it near a humidifier, on a pebble tray, or by frequent misting.

TEMPERATURE
They do not like cold environments and prefer temperatures from 65–77°F (18–25°C). Temperatures above and below these can cause damage to the plant, first evident in the curling of healthy leaves. Keep away from drafts and indoor heating sources.

PESTS
Spider mites are the most common pests. The best method to get rid of them is to wash all the leaves and stems with a gentle stream of water, then wipe with a mixture

of castile soap and water, and finally rinse again with water. (To make your own insecticidal soap spray, combine 1 Tbsp. (15ml) of castile soap with 3 oz. (1 L) of water; shake well and use immediately.) I find this method works every time. Neem oil does not agree with calatheas—it will cause the leaves to turn yellow and fall off!

QUICK CARE TIPS

- Position in bright indirect light to maintain healthy and vibrant leaf color.
- Water when the top 2" (5cm) of soil have dried out. Never allow the soil to completely dry out or be soaking wet. Calatheas like moist soil!
- Keep in temperatures from 65–77°F (18–25°C).
- Increase humidity with frequent misting, a humidifier, or a pebble tray.

Look out for:

- Browning, yellowing or curling leaves, an indication the plant needs watering.
- Drooping or rotting stems, caused by one of two things: overwatering or cold temperatures.
- Brown leaf tips and edges, caused by tap water (use only distilled water or rainwater) or lack of humidity.

TILLANDSIA (AIR PLANT)

Tillandsia are not conventional houseplants, but they have grown in popularity among enthusiasts and have now become available to purchase in many shops. Native to deserts, mountains, and forests of South and Central America, they will be found growing clinging on to tree trunks, bushes, shrubs, and rocks. Tillandsia are more commonly known as air plants because they do not require soil to grow. This has attracted plant lovers to explore the wonders of air plants, but don't be fooled! Just because no soil is required doesn't mean they are necessarily easy to care for.

Air plants are fascinating to look at, and in my opinion there really is no other indoor plant quite like them. They come in many shapes, sizes, and varieties with furry, fuzzy, spiky, or long-trailing foliage so there is an air plant to suit everyone's taste. I particularly love their air-purifying qualities.

Air plants can be placed in terrariums or attached to pretty much anything. I particularly love attaching them to driftwood to create an eye-catching rustic display. If you are looking for an unusual plant, air plants are worth having a go as they will surely add a fun, trendy look to any space.

Larger, trailing air plants are best shown off hanging, while smaller varieties will look great on a shelf or side table. For working environments, consider brightening your work space with an air plant on the desk.

Given the right care conditions, air plants can produce dainty flowers, which are always so delightful and rewarding. Depending on the species these cute blooms can last from a few days to a few months, displaying bright colors such as red, pink, and purple. With all of the love and attention you have given your air plant, do bear in mind that flowering is the end of its life cycle so after flowering it will eventually die. But it's not all bad—your efforts caring for this "diva" have paid off as you were able to see it to maturity and be rewarded with blooming!

POSITION

Air plants thrive in bright indirect light. Left in direct sunlight they will lose too much moisture and dry up.

WATERING

Air plants do not have roots like other plants; their tiny roots are designed to cling on to other plants and tree trunks in the wild. They draw in moisture and nutrients from the environment. When grown indoors the correct way to ensure your plant has absorbed enough moisture is to submerge it in a jar of water and let it soak for around 30 minutes, then gently give the plant a shake to get rid of excess water. Afterward, place upside down on a towel to dry. Do this once a week.

FEEDING

Since air plants take nutrients from the environment, feeding will be minimal. Feed once every 3–4 months using a liquid fertilizer diluted to one-quarter the strength recommended on the product label. Pour the diluted fertilizer into a spray bottle and lightly spray over the plant (do this at a time when it is due to be watered, that way you water and feed at the same time).

HUMIDITY

Most homes are not humid enough for air plants, especially during the winter months. You can provide them with the extra humidity they need by misting every couple of days or alternatively displaying them in the bathroom.

TEMPERATURE

Air plants grow best in temperatures from 50–86°F (10–30°C). They are very sensitive to extreme cold.

PESTS

Air plants are commonly infected by mealybugs and scale insects, which are usually found around the stems and leaves. Pests are mostly attracted to a dying plant! If it is healthy and has been infected with pests, simply submerge in water or rinse well under running water. Most often this is enough to dislodge and eliminate them.

QUICK CARE TIPS

- Silver varieties are more drought tolerant, while greener varieties will require more moisture.
- Get creative and make your own mini plant world by displaying smaller air plants in a terrarium.

Look out for:

- Browning leaf tips, an indication the plant needs more water.
- Browning, soggy-looking leaves, an indication the plant has been overwatered.

QUICK CARE TIPS

- Increase humidity around the plant using a pebble tray or frequent misting. Consider displaying in the bathroom.
- Do not touch the delicate leaves with your hands as the plant is very sensitive.
- Keep in bright indirect light; avoid direct sunlight.
- Keep the soil evenly moist, never soaking wet. Do not allow it to dry out.

Look out for:

Spores. A healthy, mature maidenhair fern will develop spores on the leaves. They look like brown dots, so don't panic: these are not pests and your plant is not dying! It is happy and healthy, and you have successfully grown the plant to its mature state.

ADIANTUM (MAIDENHAIR FERN)

Native to the Himalayas, adiantum is more commonly known as the maidenhair fern. In my experience—and I'm sure many plant lovers will agree—this is the hardest out of all ferns to care for indoors. No matter how many times I tried over the years, I could never get it right. Now, after years of experience with this gorgeous delicate fern, I can share with you how to successfully grow this "diva."

Maidenhair ferns can be found in many different sizes. Larger ones are best suited in hanging baskets as they can grow very bushy, while smaller ferns would look stunning clustered among other humidity-loving plants on a shelf to add a delicate, whimsical touch of green. They are semi-evergreen with dark stems and finely divided fronds. Their tiny leaves are fan shaped and tissue thin, and look so divinely elegant.

They are very sensitive, so although it's tempting to touch the gorgeous leaves, I wouldn't as even the warmth and oils from our skin can damage them. This plant really is a diva!

While growing the maidenhair fern indoors is definitely tricky, if you make the commitment to provide all of its care needs you will be forever delighted with its lush, fluffy foliage.

POSITION
Keep in bright indirect light. They are happiest near a window but out of harsh sunlight, which will scorch their delicate leaves.

WATERING
Keep the soil moist. The golden rule is never allow the soil to dry out. Otherwise, the fronds will brown and shrivel. Be careful not to overwater as they do not like soggy soil either.

SOIL MIX
Use a rich, well-draining potting soil. I like to put damp sphagnum moss as a top dressing for my maidenhair ferns to help retain moisture and they love it!

FEEDING
Feed once a month throughout the year using a dilutable liquid fertilizer. I would suggest using half the recommended strength stated on the bottle to ensure the plant doesn't suffer leaf burn. This works for me as it's always better to underfeed, and as maidenhair ferns are such divas it's better to be cautious.

HUMIDITY
They love humidity. Place on a tray of pebbles and mist daily. Maidenhair ferns make a great choice to display in the bathroom, too, since the air gets humid from baths and showers.

TEMPERATURE
Maidenhair ferns thrive in moderately warm, humid environments. The ideal temperature is from 60–70°F (15–21°C). Do not allow temperatures to drop below 50°F (10°C) during the winter months. Keep away from drafts and radiators.

PESTS
Aphids are attracted to the maidenhair fern. If they occur, simply hose off the fronds with a gentle stream of water.

CURIO ROWLEYANUS (STRING OF PEARLS)

Curio rowleyanus is commonly known as the string of pearls because it resembles a beaded necklace with its plump, pea-like foliage. Native to South Africa, it grows as a creeping vine, rooting itself along the ground. String of pearls is notoriously hard to care for, but that hasn't stopped it from growing in popularity as an indoor plant. I have seen many posts on social media showing off the string of pearls and its quirky appearance; then weeks later a post update where the plant has shrivelled up and withered away. The key element to get right when it comes to caring for this plant is watering.

It is best displayed in a hanging basket, allowing the divine pearl-like foliage to gracefully spill over the side of the pot and dangle down freely. Having the string of pearls hanging from a basket will add visual interest to any indoor setting.

Given the right care, the string of pearls is a fast-growing succulent vine with a mature length of 12"–24" (30–60cm). If you find that your plant is balding at the top, this is because there isn't enough light shining down on to the crown. To make it fuller, simply trim and add the cuttings back into the top of the pot. These cuttings will root into the soil within a few weeks to create a bushier plant.

POSITION

String of pearls requires between 6 and 8 hours of bright light a day. Placing near a sunny window will keep it happy and reward you with new plump, pearl-like foliage.

WATERING

Watering is very often where people go wrong. This is a succulent, which means it stores water in its foliage. Succulents always need less watering than other indoor plants. Water about once every 2 weeks. A good rule of thumb is to check the top layer of soil; push your finger in, and if the top half-inch is dry, then it's time for a drink.

SOIL MIX

Choose a succulent or cactus potting mix.

FEEDING

Feed once a month during the growing season with fish emulsion (organic plant food high in nitrogen produced from the remains of fish that would otherwise go to waste) or a very diluted liquid fertilizer. Dilute either of these to one-quarter the strength recommended on the product label. In my experience, the fish emulsion encourages vigorous growth with lush green foliage.

HUMIDITY

String of pearls thrives in average humidity levels, so avoid places like the bathroom or kitchen.

TEMPERATURE

It cannot tolerate cold temperatures; aim for around 72°F (22°C).

PESTS

Common pests are mealybugs, aphids, scale insects, spider mites, and fungus gnats. These pests can easily be eradicated by spraying with insecticidal soap. See page 118 for a homemade insecticidal soap recipe.

CURIO X PEREGRINUS (STRING OF DOLPHINS)

This succulent is commonly known as string of dolphins as its unusual leaves perfectly resemble a pod of little jumping dolphins. It is native to South America and is in fact a hybrid between *Curio articulatus* (candle plant) and *Curio rowleyanus* (string of pearls). (The × in the name indicates a cross or hybrid between two species.) String of dolphins grows in dry climates so average room temperatures and humidity are ideal.

It is a rare plant, though I have seen it grow in popularity on social media as people are fascinated with the cute dolphin-shaped leaves. String of dolphins can grow up to 36" (90cm) long and 6" (15cm) tall. When you see this plant, you cannot help but fall in love with it instantly. But make no mistake: in my experience it is tricky to care for. However, do not be put off by the challenge as the string of dolphins will bring joy to any indoor space. As a trailing succulent, displaying in a hanging basket works best and looks stunning.

Considering how hard it can be to find this plant in shops and how tricky it is to care for, I particularly love how easy it is to propagate. Simply take a stem cutting with at least 6 nodes (the nodes can be found at the points where the leaves emerge and are where the roots will grow). Remove two dolphin-shaped leaves from the cut end and place in water. Roots should develop in a couple of weeks.

I always like to propagate divas and rare plants; that way I will have a backup if my mother plant dies or gets a really bad infestation. I call it plant insurance!

POSITION
Place in bright indirect light. Wherever the location is, make sure that the light is coming from above and shining down on to the crown of the plant. This will prevent it from balding on the top.

WATERING
Allow the soil to dry out in between watering—ensure that the pot feels light first. Succulents store a lot of water in the leaves so be careful not to overwater. With all succulents I use the bottom-up method by placing the pot on a saucer of water so that it is 25 percent submerged. Allow the roots to suck up as much water as the plant needs; that way you won't overwater. Let it sit in the water for 5–15 minutes or until the top of the soil feels slightly damp to the touch; refill the saucer with water if needed.

SOIL MIX
Use a well-draining soil. I recommend using a cactus or succulent mix. Alternatively, you can make your own by combining 2 parts regular potting soil with 1 part perlite and 1 part coarse sand.

FEEDING
It does not require regular feeding. Overfeeding can cause the leaves to lose their iconic dolphin shape. I would suggest only feeding once in early spring to boost growth using a liquid fertilizer diluted as recommended on the product label.

HUMIDITY
Average indoor humidity levels are fine for this plant.

TEMPERATURE
Unlike other succulents, string of dolphins loves cool air and withstands indoor temperatures as low as 41°F (5°C).

PESTS
Common pests are aphids, scale insects, mealybugs, and spider mites. To get rid of any pests, simply use a cotton swab dipped in rubbing alcohol.

QUICK CARE TIPS

- Remember when positioned in bright indirect light to make sure the crown of the plant is getting light to prevent the top from going bald.

- When watering succulents, use the bottom-up method to ensure you don't overwater and allow the soil to dry in between.

- Propagate to create a new string of dolphins—it's easy in water.

BEGONIA REX

Native to northeastern India, southern China, and Vietnam, rex (or king) begonia has become a popular indoor plant and is widely available in shops and garden centers; I have even come across it in my local supermarket.

This is a stunning plant that is mostly grown for its fancy foliage. The leaves can be found in many different shades of green, red, purple, and pink with slight hints of metallic silver, making it so unusual and eye-catching. It does flower but the blooms are insignificant.

Make no mistake, this plant is hard to care for. I have found it to be a real diva. Literally, all of the conditions have to be *perfect* in order for it to thrive.

POSITION

It requires bright indirect light; direct sun exposure will scorch its delicate leaves. Note that it can be toxic to pets and humans so take this into account when positioning it in your home.

WATERING

When watering I would suggest rainwater or distilled water, because tap water with high levels of mineral salts will cause the leaf edges to burn. I keep the watering schedule simple when it comes to this plant: water weekly when the top inch of the soil becomes dry. (If watering day arrives and the top inch of soil is not yet dry, hold off and check the next day.) Do be careful not to get the foliage wet as this can cause disease and the leaves to shrivel.

SOIL MIX

The number one thing to get right is that the soil must be light, rich, and well draining. Adding perlite to your potting mix will definitely help with drainage and keep your plant happy. Also make sure that the pot has adequate drainage holes.

FEEDING

Feed with a diluted organic soluble fertilizer (half strength) every 2–3 weeks in the growing season.

HUMIDITY

It appreciates an environment of around 50 percent humidity, so placing on a pebble tray or near a humidifier would be great. Misting to raise the humidity would be detrimental as this would cause powdery mildew. Think about where the best position would be— for example, you wouldn't want to place it around the plants that require misting.

TEMPERATURE

Begonia rex thrives in temperatures from 59–70°F (15–21°C). Note that it will stop growing when temperatures fall below 57°F (14°C) so keep away from drafty windows.

PESTS

It can occasionally be troubled by mealybugs. If an infestation occurs, to remove them simply brush the pests directly with a cotton swab dipped in alcohol.

With a little more care and attention, and my tips, you can successfully grow these "diva plants" with confidence.

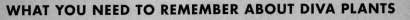

WHAT YOU NEED TO REMEMBER ABOUT DIVA PLANTS

- All the plants in this category are tricky to care for. If you are a new plant parent, I would suggest waiting until you have more experience before adding one to your indoor garden.

- Check before you buy whether a plant is "high maintenance."

- Pay close attention to lighting, watering, humidity, temperature, soil, and feeding.

- Be prepared to move these plants around the home/office at first until you have found the perfect location where they will thrive.

- Expect sudden leaf drop (even on healthy leaves). This is very common in plants when they are adapting to their new environment.

- Use rainwater not tap water, which has chemicals such as chloride and fluoride that can build up in the soil and damage roots, and will eventually kill the plant.

Photographing Plants for Social Media

Indoor plants have increasingly boomed on social media. Gardening, especially indoor gardening, has never been trendier. Plant lovers are sharing their passion with their friends and followers more than ever before, encouraging a new generation of green fingers. Those who follow plant accounts on social media will have noticed that they come and go out of fashion very quickly. I have seen this happen with the string of pearls, string of dolphins, and the Chinese money plant, to name a few. It's quite sad to see as I remember a time when, for example, you couldn't find a Chinese money plant anywhere because of the huge demand for them—fast forward a few months and they were everywhere in shops looking tired, neglected, and forgotten. All plants need a home and are all individually beautiful in their own unique ways, no matter how popular or unpopular they may be. Try not to get drawn into the "fashion" of plants. Remember that they are living things, deserve the care and attention they require, and are worth much more than a social media beauty shot.

Whether you're keeping records of houseplant growth or just simply blown away at how stunning a leaf looks, for keen plant parents wanting to photograph their plant pets here are some quick tips to capture their beauty and essence.

ABOVE *Cleistocactus strausii* (silver torch cactus); *Opuntia monacantha* (prickly pear); *Echinocactus grusonii* (golden barrel cactus).

OPPOSITE *Nepenthes* 'Gaya' (tropical pitcher plant).

1 LIGHTING

Always opt for natural lighting when photographing indoor plants as it shows off their natural beauty. Photographing plants indoors can be tricky because of low light levels; I suggest moving closer to the window or even quickly stepping outside. I would avoid adding filters to photos as you lose the true natural essence of the plant.

2 FOLIAGE

Plants have the most stunning foliage displaying delightful colored leaves, some patterned and textured. Try zooming in and getting a close-up shot of the leaf pattern and texture. We don't often pay close attention to fine details of leaf veins, etc. You will be surprised what you can capture with a zoomed-in leaf photo.

3 COLOR AND PATTERN

Add color to your plant shots with decorative colorful pots. I like to match my plants with my pots; for example, darker foliage always looks lush in a light-colored pot. Plants with patterned foliage look better in a plain pot as opposed to one with a bold pattern. Let the leaves do the talking!

4 COMPOSITION

Clustering plants together as a group shot always looks marvellous. Pay attention to objects in the background and choose plants that complement each other.

Plants are being captured on camera more and more, so give it a shot and show off the beauty of your indoor plants!

5 SCALE

Get creative and capture the miniature world of succulents in terrariums, clustered in bowls, or clustered on shelves (aka "shelfies").

6 DOCUMENT

Rescued a plant from the brink of death? Take "before and after" photos.

LEFT Here I have planted the humidity-loving fittonia in a terrarium.

OPPOSITE *Tradescantia* 'Nanouk Pink' (fantasy Venice); *Alocasia* x *amazonica* (Alocasia 'Polly').

Taking Care of Your Indoor Garden during the Winter Months

Winter can be a tricky time for plant parents, and winter plant care often gets overlooked. We can get used to our spring/summer schedules and continue the same care habits during the winter months, which should be avoided. Watering will be less frequent and feeding should be reduced for the vast majority of indoor plants. Use room temperature as opposed to cold water to avoid shocking the roots.

The days are shorter during the winter, which means less light for our indoor plants. You may consider having grow lights for some of your plants so that they get the light they require. Frequently wipe the foliage using a damp cloth to remove dust to ensure they can absorb what light there is more easily.

It's important to remember that they are not actively growing at this time. Most plants generally slow down their growth while some, such as caladiums, go completely into dormancy. It's hard for us plant parents to see a cherished specimen drop its leaves altogether as it becomes dormant.

One thing I would like to mention is indoor heating. Heating appliances can have a real impact on our indoor gardens, with the sudden drop and rise in temperatures causing our plants stress. I suggest moving plants away from drafty windows, air vents, and radiators to protect them from perishing. Also pay attention to soil media drying out more quickly now that the heating is on! If you're lucky enough to have underfloor heating, move floor plants off the ground on to a stand so that the roots don't get too warm.

Consider misting your humidity-loving plants more frequently as the air is more likely to be dry in a warm, heated indoor environment. Pebble trays and humidifiers work very well.

A nice warm and cosy indoor setting provides the perfect environment for pests like aphids, mealybugs, spider mites, and thrips to thrive and breed over winter. Frequently check your plants, especially under the leaves. Remove any dried or dead leaves to help prevent mold and mildew and get rid of lurking pests.

With these few winter plant care tips, I am confident your indoor garden will see through the cold and dark months and will bounce back with vitality to bring you even more joy in spring!

Index

Acknowledgments

My infinite appreciation to all at Pimpernel Press for their support, especially Carey Smith for her guidance and patience throughout the whole process; without her I would not have had this opportunity to write my first book. Thanks also to Becky Clarke for her contribution to the layout and design, and choosing all of my best photos for the book. Also thank you to Nancy Marten for her eye for detail when painstakingly reading through my text, making sure I have dotted all the I's and crossed all the T's.

A huge thank you to my dear friend Mark C. Bolton, who helped me remain calm and grounded throughout this whole project, always being that voice I needed to hear to keep me pushing through.

Thank you to Monty Don for his encouraging personal message.

A massive thank you to Chine Home for supplying and delivering stunning plant specimens to feature in the book; you really have been amazing to work with.

Thank you to the Slingsby family for allowing me to use their beautiful home for a backdrop when photographing the plants. You really have been so accommodating.

Last but not least, thank you to Ronan Keating, who hand delivered my *Dracaena marginata* that is featured in the book (see page 29).

And finally, as a child I would bingewatch David Attenborough's nature programs and now as an adult he has become my hero: I will forever be inspired by him.

A huge thank you to the following companies for supplying plants, pots, and location, without which this book would not have been possible.

Chine Home (suppliers of plants and pots)
@Chine.kensalrise on Instagram
70 Chamberlayne Road, London NW10 3JJ

Jen's Plants and Florist (suppliers of plants)
@jensplantsandflorist on Instagram
106 Brick Lane, London E1 6RL

Southern Grove Real Estate (location for plant photography)
www.southerngrove.co.uk
@southerngrove on Instagram

About the Author

Having studied Art & Design and Photography at William Morris Academy in London, Jade Murray began nurturing her creative flair by starting her own indoor garden. Jade has always held all elements of nature close to her heart. In 2021, she entered the Royal Horticultural Society "My Chelsea Garden" virtual competition (in partnership with BBC's *The One Show*) and wowed the judges, who were so impressed by her achievements they awarded her the Judges' Choice gold medal.

Jade believes that plants contribute to our peace of mind and has a special bond with them. Her aim is to encourage all generations to incorporate plants into their lives, not only to create calming spaces indoors, but also to show how caring for plants can be beneficial to our mental health. In her spare time Jade enjoys the outdoors and visiting garden centers. Her dream would be to open up her own plant shop and spread plant love to all. She lives in West London with her three children, who find plants as rewarding as she does.

Jade shares her knowledge and plant care tips online @PlantAvenueW10 on Instagram.